Brad Pitt

Titles in the People in the News series include:

PEOPLE
IN THE NEWS

Brad Pitt

by Terri Dougherty

Lucent Books, San Diego, CA

For my family, especially my husband, Denis, whose help on this book was invaluable.

Library of Congress Cataloging-in-Publication Data

Dougherty, Terri
  Brad Pitt / by Terri Dougherty.
    p. cm. — (People in the news)
  Includes bibliographical references and index.
  ISBN 1-56006-867-1 (hardback. : alk. paper)
  1. Pitt, Brad, 1963—Juvenile literature. 2. Motion picture actors and actresses—United States—Biography—Juvenile literature. [1. Pitt, Brad, 1963— . 2. Actors and actresses.] I. Title. II. People in the news (San Diego, Calif.)
  PN2287.P54 D68 2002
  791.43'028'092—dc21

00–013095

Table of Contents

Foreword

FAME AND CELEBRITY are alluring. People are drawn to those who walk in fame's spotlight, whether they are known for great accomplishments or for notorious deeds. The lives of the famous pique public interest and attract attention, perhaps because their experiences seem in some ways so different from, yet in other ways so similar to, our own.

Newspapers, magazines, and television regularly capitalize on this fascination with celebrity by running profiles of famous people. For example, television programs such as *Entertainment Tonight* devote all of their programming to stories about entertainment and entertainers. Magazines such as *People* fill their pages with stories of the private lives of famous people. Even newspapers, newsmagazines, and television news frequently delve into the lives of well-known personalities. Despite the number of articles and programs, few provide more than a superficial glimpse at their subjects.

Lucent's People in the News series offers young readers a deeper look into the lives of today's newsmakers, the influences that have shaped them, and the impact they have had in their fields of endeavor and on other people's lives. The subjects of the series hail from many disciplines and walks of life. They include authors, musicians, athletes, political leaders, entertainers, entrepreneurs, and others who have made a mark on modern life and who, in many cases, will continue to do so for years to come.

These biographies are more than factual chronicles. Each book emphasizes the contributions, accomplishments, or deeds that have brought fame or notoriety to the individual and shows how that person has influenced modern life. Authors portray their subjects in a realistic, unsentimental light. For example, Bill Gates—the cofounder and chief executive officer of the software giant Microsoft—has been instrumental in making personal computers the most vital tool of the modern age. Few dispute his business savvy, his perseverance, or his technical expertise, yet critics say he is ruthless in his dealings with competitors and driven more by his desire to maintain Microsoft's dominance in the computer industry than by an interest in furthering technology.

In these books, young readers will encounter inspiring stories about real people who achieved success despite enormous obstacles. Oprah Winfrey—the most powerful, most watched, and wealthiest woman on television today—spent the first six years of her life in the care of her grandparents while her unwed mother sought work and a better life elsewhere. Her adolescence was colored by promiscuity, pregnancy at age fourteen, rape, and sexual abuse.

Each author documents and supports his or her work with an array of primary and secondary source quotations taken from diaries, letters, speeches, and interviews. All quotes are footnoted to show readers exactly how and where biographers derive their information and provide guidance for further research. The quotations enliven the text by giving readers eyewitness views of the life and accomplishments of each person covered in the People in the News series.

In addition, each book in the series includes photographs, annotated bibliographies, timelines, and comprehensive indexes. For both the casual reader and the student researcher, the People in the News series offers insight into the lives of today's newsmakers—people who shape the way we live, work, and play in the modern age.

Introduction

Working His Way to the Top

B RAD PITT HAS captivated audiences since a small role in 1991's *Thelma and Louise* showed the world his outward good looks and his inner fire. Intriguing and beguiling, Pitt can't escape the fact that his early career was driven by his attractive features, and his name has become synonymous with good-looking. He is the ultimate male pinup, with a well-toned body, piercing blue eyes, and provocative lips. Yet underneath his well-proportioned exterior is a man determined to succeed on another level.

Pitt isn't content to have a career that rests solely upon public adoration of his good looks. He has constantly refined his image to prove to the world that there is substance beneath his handsome physique. Determined to be recognized for his acting, he worked on his craft and improved. A look at his early films shows how far he has come. The forced gestures and mumbled dialogue in *The Dark Side of the Sun*, made in 1988, and clumsy on-screen chemistry in *The Favor*, made in 1991, are in stark contrast to his Golden Globe–winning performance in *12 Monkeys* (1995) and his engaging portrayal of the menacing Tyler Durden in *Fight Club* (1999).

Always looking to improve and stretch his acting career, Pitt has stayed away from one-dimensional characters and movies that are little more than excuses to put his handsome face on the screen. Pitt has shown that he has the ability to succeed in diverse roles, taking on parts as a depressed vampire opposite Tom Cruise in *Interview with the Vampire*, a hotshot detective in *Seven*, and a wild, charming, and troubled son in *A River Runs Through It*.

Good Looks Not Good Enough

Pitt always knew he had the looks, but he also knew they weren't enough. His handsome features might have been his biggest asset when he left the University of Missouri two credits shy of graduation to see what Hollywood had to offer, but his looks could have been a detriment to his career if he had let roles that relied on appearance rule his decisions. Pitt was so determined to achieve success through his acting that he deliberately downplayed his good looks in movies like *Kalifornia* and *Fight Club* and in public hid behind a beard and long hair.

Twice named *People Weekly*'s Sexiest Man Alive, Pitt is certainly no stranger to accolades for his winsome features, but he's desirable as much for his inner character as his exterior assets. He's engaging and charming, with a charisma that is captured by the camera. Pitt knows how to impress people and has an instinct for winning people over. When a college friend loaned him her class notes, he sent her a thank-you gift of flowers. The cast of *Growing Pains* received

Brad Pitt has come a long way since his supporting role in the 1991 film The Favor, *which was panned by critics.*

a basket of muffins from Pitt after he appeared on the sitcom early in his career. He romanced his wife, actress Jennifer Aniston, with an extravagant birthday celebration in Mexico.

Pitt has led an intriguing personal life. His romances with costars have provided plenty of fodder for tabloids, but he's been very serious and committed when in a relationship. He set up housekeeping with Juliette Lewis, was engaged to Gwyneth Paltrow, and married Aniston. Although his romances were well documented in newspapers and magazines, Pitt prefers quiet evenings at home to glamorous Hollywood events.

Independence Pays Off for Pitt

Pitt's life in Hollywood is far removed from his ordinary upbringing in Springfield, Missouri. Fiercely independent, Pitt's desire for individualism drove him away from a life he considered mundane to an exciting chance to challenge the unknown. Although he became a Hollywood superstar, he brought part of his childhood with him. Pitt hasn't forgotten his Missouri roots, traveling back home every year at Christmas and investing in land around his hometown. The principles he learned in childhood have remained with him throughout his career, as he relies on an inbred sense of fairness to do what he thinks is best.

The independent streak that led Pitt away from Missouri kept him grounded in Hollywood. Determined not to give in to Hollywood stereotypes, Pitt has chosen roles that are challenging and go against his image as a young stud. In this manner, he improved his ability as an actor and his drawing power at the box office. Some of his decisions have brought him accolades and box office success, such as his supporting role in *12 Monkeys*. Some have been critical disappointments, such as *Seven Years in Tibet*. Whatever the outcome of his decisions, by selecting diverse and interesting projects, he has proven himself an individual of strong disposition.

When Pitt makes a decision that doesn't turn out as he expects, he doesn't let it get him down. He knows he might make the wrong choice, but he is willing to face it and move on. When times are tough, he remains confident that success and happiness will inevitably follow. He works hard on the job, even when

Pitt smiles after winning a Golden Globe Award for his supporting role in 12 Monkeys.

he's not happy with the way a film is going. He is admired for his attitude toward hard work and applauded for the result that hard work brings to the screen.

Pitt's tenaciously positive attitude has been rewarded with a successful career and happy marriage. Contending with fame isn't easy, yet Pitt remains likable. He's sometimes brooding but always optimistic. He has a strong belief in himself that carries over to the characters he portrays on the screen. He's comfortable with himself and at peace with the decisions he's made. That self-confidence comes across on the screen and makes audiences want to get to know him better.

Chapter 1

Solid Foundation

When William Bradley Pitt was born on December 18, 1963, in Shawnee, Oklahoma, his parents couldn't have guessed that the darling baby they were holding in their arms would one day become a Hollywood hunk twice dubbed the Sexiest Man Alive.

Proud parents Bill and Jane Pitt were far removed from the lights of Hollywood. There was no show business blood running in their midwestern veins. Bill worked as a truck driver and later managed a trucking company, and Jane was a high school counselor. They prized hard work and their Baptist religion and wanted to pass their values on to the son they called Brad.

Brad respected his parents and the values they tried to instill in him. His solid upbringing served him well years later as he stayed grounded amid fast-paced Hollywood lifestyles. When his chiseled body, sparkling blue eyes, and engaging smile brought him fame and fortune, he gave his parents credit for being the most important guides in his life.

Moving to Missouri

Soon after Brad was born, his family moved from the center of Oklahoma to Springfield, Missouri, about 250 miles to the northeast. His father saw better job opportunities in the larger city of Springfield, so Bill, Jane, and their young son headed to a new home in the shadow of the Ozark Mountains.

Springfield, home to 156,000 people, is the third largest city in Missouri, behind Kansas City and St. Louis. Built on the Ozark Plateau in the southwest corner of the state, the city is surrounded by lush, wooded rolling hills and clear blue lakes, rivers, and spring-fed streams. The scenic region is a favorite spot for tourists who enjoy camping, canoeing, and fishing. Temperatures reach an average low of twenty-one degrees in January and peak at an average of eighty-nine degrees on sunny days in July, giving the city four distinctive seasons for its residents to enjoy. Brad grew to love and cherish the region. Even after he moved to the Los Angeles area, he visited his home on holidays and bought land in Missouri. He and his father developed a subdivision there, with a goal of creating a community of homes on spacious tracts of land in harmony with nature.

Strong Family Ties

Springfield is still the home of Brad's parents, brother, and sister. Brad's brother, Doug, came into the world three years after Brad was born. Their sister, Julie, was born two years later. The trio remains close. Doug, a businessman who owns a computer company, helped shield details about Brad and Jennifer Aniston's wedding from the press and isn't overwhelmed by his brother's superstar status. Doug and Julie have families of their own in Springfield. Julie

A scenic view of Wilson's Creek Battlefield National Park near Springfield, Missouri, the city where Pitt grew up and his family still lives.

Brad's Springfield

Brad Pitt grew up in Springfield, Missouri, a city with a rich history and a beautiful rural setting. Springfield, which was settled in about 1830, became a city in 1847. Missouri was the site of many Civil War battles, and the bloody battle of Wilson's Creek was fought near Springfield. More than twenty-three hundred Confederate and Union soldiers were killed or wounded in the battle. The battle site is now home to the Wilson Creek Battlefield National Park. Confederate and Union soldiers are buried in Springfield National Cemetery.

The Mark Twain National Forest, south of Springfield, offered young Brad an outlet for hiking and horseback riding in one of the largest national forests in the United States. Crystal Caverns, the Ozark Wonder Cave, and the Fantastic Cavern near Springfield gave him opportunities to explore unusual rock formations.

In the 1970s Springfield's population hovered around 120,000, making it then, as now, the third-largest city in the state. It was an important city in the lumbering and mining industries, as well as in farming. The importance of farming was evident in the city's businesses. Springfield was home to one of the largest dairy processing plants in the country, and flour mills and meatpacking plants were also major businesses in town. Kraft Foods continues to be a major employer in Springfield and for years has employed people in the production of sauces, pasta, and cheese products. When Brad was young, electronics equipment plants, machine shops, and trailer factories also provided jobs for residents. The city's colleges included Central Bible, Drury, Evangel, and Southwest Missouri State.

The Frisco Railroad, now remembered in a Springfield museum, intersected the town while Brad was growing up. Several major highways pass through Springfield, including U.S. 60, U.S. 160, U.S. 65, and Interstate 44, making it a natural hub for trucking businesses like the one Brad's father managed.

Antique shops abound in small towns near Springfield. As an adult Brad filled his Hollywood mansion with antiques, perhaps feeding an interest in historic objects that was fueled by the antique stores that were so plentiful near his hometown.

Although Pitt didn't participate in theater in his youth, Springfield boasted a fine playhouse, the Landers Theatre. Built in 1909, it is still in operation and is the home of the Springfield Little Theatre. The Springfield Art Museum offered another cultural outlet. Located next to Phelps Grove Park, it hosts a nationally renowned watercolor exhibit each summer.

credits their solid upbringing with giving her brother the inner strength he needed to become a successful actor. Brad always had a way with people and from an early age was successful in his pursuits.

Brad's likable personality came through during his childhood. At Horace Mann Elementary School in Springfield, Brad was a nice kid who got along well with his peers. He is remembered as a sweet, polite, somewhat quiet little boy with big blue eyes and dimples. He had enough confidence in himself to know that he didn't have to show off in order to be noticed.

Brad's star qualities were apparent at home as well. His mother recognized that there was something special about her charismatic firstborn son. Brad says she was the first person to see he had a knack for entertaining people. She influenced her son's captivating personality, while his father passed on his handsome features. "Brad looks like his father, and he has the personality of his mother," said one of Brad's best friends from college, Chris Schudy. "His mother is so down-to-earth, just a super woman. His dad is a great guy but more reserved." [1]

Showing Some Talent

The family's involvement at South Haven Baptist Church gave Brad an early opportunity to showcase his charm and talent. When he sang in the church choir, the eyes of those watching were drawn to him. "You couldn't keep from watching Brad because his face was so expressive," said Connie Bilyeu, a pianist at the church who became Brad's high school drama coach. "He would move his little mouth so big with all the words that he attracted everyone's attention." [2]

Brad didn't stand out quite as much in plays produced by the church. He was a member of the supporting casts but stayed away from lead roles. He avoided the spotlight, preferring to participate without being the star.

Acting took a backseat to religion and family for the Pitts. Although Bill Pitt's job kept him on the road regularly, he maintained strong ties with his children. When possible, he took them on the road with him, showing them the world outside Springfield that Brad would yearn to see more of after college.

Bill Pitt's dedication to his job instilled in his son the values of commitment and hard work. Bill Pitt modeled the values that would later help Brad dedicate himself to learning the craft of acting. Working hard six days a week for thirty-six years, Bill Pitt displayed a devotion to his job that was not lost on his son. He was a hard worker who was also there when his family needed him.

If Brad overstepped his bounds, his dad was there to rein him in. When Brad was a teenager, he threw a tantrum while playing in a tennis tournament. Screaming and throwing a racket were not qualities Bill Pitt wanted Brad to display, and he had his son rethink his actions by making him take a fresh look at them. Brad's father approached him on the court between games. "He just said, 'Are you having fun?'" Brad said. "I got all huffy and said no. He looked at me and said, 'Then don't do it.' And then he walked away. Boy, that put me in my place."[3]

A Desire to See the World

Brad had a happy childhood in Springfield, but he was also intensely interested in the world around him. The trips he took with his father let him glimpse other parts of the country, and movies and music brought the outside world into his hometown.

Films gave Brad a look at other places and lifestyles. In 1977, at age thirteen, he saw John Travolta disco dancing in *Saturday*

Respecting His Family's Privacy

As Brad's career blossomed, he became more reluctant to discuss his family or the details of his childhood. He always made it clear that he had a happy, easygoing life as a child but hesitated to participate in lengthy discussions. Brad didn't want to expose his family to the life in the spotlight he had chosen for himself.

While he avoided lengthy narratives on the topic, Brad did offer a few choice details to reporters. When writer Chris Heath asked him, for an article in *Rolling Stone*, what smell reminded him of his childhood, Pitt replied, "A nice big fart." He told Jancee Dunn of *Rolling Stone* that he had his first drink in the basement of the family's home in Springfield, when he snuck a sip of Chivas. He also told her that the first concert he ever saw was the Doobie Brothers, with Foreigner opening.

After seeing the movie Saturday Night Fever *at age thirteen, Pitt was determined to one day leave the comfort of his hometown to see the world.*

Night Fever. The street life portrayed in the film made him realize how different the world could be outside of his comfortable family life in Springfield. Something inside told him he'd leave Missouri one day, even though he loved his hometown. He wanted to see more of the world he saw on television and in movies and read about in books.

Brad was also impressed by the emotions movies could stir in him. When he saw the 1968 movie *Planet of the Apes* in a rerelease at the drive-in with his parents, he was amazed by the impact of the movie's final scene. When Charlton Heston sees the Statue of Liberty and realizes the planet being run by apes is really Earth, Brad's eyes were also opened to a new world.

A typical teen, Brad also enjoyed popular music. Saving his money to buy records, he liked the songs of Elton John and the Who's *Tommy.* His tastes reflected the choices of many teenagers at the time but sometimes conflicted with what he heard on the radio. "When I was growing up, we had only the Top 40 country songs on the radio," he said. "They figured that's all we'd listen to, but if we'd been offered something else, it would have been accepted. It's a little like a closed society. You can only experience what's available."[4]

Practicing guitar in his bedroom, he dreamed of being a rock star. He also calculated his chances of someday being in the movies. "I thought, 'If I'd been born in California, I'd have a shot at them,'" he said. "Then you realize you can go there."[5]

Pitt Sticks to His Code

But before Brad left for California as an adult, he needed to nurture the qualities that would give him a foundation for success. As a child, his values were heavily influenced by his family's Baptist religion. Although he later came to think of religion as an "oppression" that stifled individual freedom, a statement he said his family was certain to disagree with, the values he learned when he was young stayed with him into adulthood.

"Pitt's got a code," said close friend Paul Feldsher. "He grew up with a code that's sort of born out of his breadbasket Christianity. In terms of morality and ethics, he's not negotiable. He has a life and an understanding of how he's meant to live that life. All this movie-star stuff is not going to deter him."[6]

Religion also left Brad searching for answers. He was troubled by the sadness he saw in the world around him and couldn't understand why God let awful things happen. He was sensitive to the state of the world around him. At times it left him feeling depressed.

"I had a very easy childhood, deprived of nothing per se," Brad said. "I just always had so many questions growing up: why this, why the state of the world, why does God want this? Congenital sadness. It always came up, for no reason. I don't know what it is."[7]

The Pitt family's ties are strong, but it wasn't easy for Brad and his family to talk about their innermost thoughts and feelings. This didn't stop the family from being warm and loving, but it meant Brad had to learn to interpret what he felt. At their home, feelings were conveyed without words. Brad became used to leaving things unsaid and had to learn to understand, discuss, and label his thoughts and feelings after he left home.

A Leader in High School

The loving home atmosphere Brad grew up with helped him do his best in high school. Brad was a good student at the 1,700-student Kickapoo High School and was a member of the debate team and student government. He had the title of public relations officer, a leadership position that got him involved in school activities.

"He was a good leader, well liked in the school cabinet, where he promoted all the dances and spirit days," said Mark Swadley, a former classmate whose father was the Pitt family's pastor. "He was very likable, never arrogant or cocky."[8]

Brad added sports to his busy high school agenda. He played tennis and basketball as a member of the Kickapoo High School

A high school yearbook photo of Pitt on the tennis team. Pitt was a popular student who played sports and was involved in debate and student government.

Chiefs. Brad also played baseball, a sport that gave him the scar on his cheek after a ball hit his face when he lost sight of a pop fly in the sun.

The scar didn't hurt his image or good looks, however. His classmates noticed his looks and style. He was named best dresser in the Kickapoo High yearbook.

Choir and drama were also part of his high school days, but his performances gave no indication that he would one day earn millions of dollars making movies. He wasn't the star of his school plays but instead had small parts in school musicals and even tried madrigal singing. Madrigal singers typically dress in medieval garb and deliver short musical poems in small groups, using minimal musical accompaniment. It takes a lot of courage and self-confidence to perform in a madrigal production, and Brad had both.

Having a Good Time

In high school Brad managed to enjoy himself while staying out of major trouble. He knew how to walk the fine line between having fun and being a delinquent. His most daring exploits included hosting "make-out parties" in his basement as a teenager. He didn't

Pitt's senior yearbook photo. After high school, Pitt majored in journalism at the University of Missouri.

quite fool his mother, however. She made a point of making a lot of noise before coming down into the basement, calling to Brad and asking if she could get a steak out of the freezer. Eventually Brad started to wonder why his mom needed to get a steak at 10 P.M., but he didn't complain when she checked up on him and his friends. He appreciated that she was setting limits without being overbearing. Years later he laughed at the memory of his mom climbing noisily down the stairs.

Brad never lacked for dates during high school and had several short-lived relationships. He knew how to turn girls' heads and capture their hearts. He wore a white tuxedo to his prom, feathering his hair back in the style of the day. He could be romantic as well as charming, as he showed one winter when he had a crush on a girl named Sara Hart. He sneaked through the snow to the area outside her classroom window and wrote "Hi Sara" and drew a heart in the snow outside her classroom.

A likable student, Brad usually got along well with his classmates. He got into one notable scuffle with another student and a teacher while in high school, throwing punches that he later regretted, but that type of conflict was rare. Brad was more likely to win people over with his charm than get into brawls with them.

Fun-Filled College Days

In 1982 Brad left high school behind and headed for the University of Missouri, in Columbia. Brad didn't stray too far from home after high school, attending college about 165 miles away. However, the distance was enough to give Brad his first taste of freedom and the good times that went along with it.

Brad majored in journalism but didn't want to become a reporter. Instead, he focused on advertising with the intention of becoming an advertising art director. He loved architecture and later thought he should have studied it seriously. At the time, however, the difficult architecture classes would have interfered with the fun he was having. "School was about getting out of classes instead of learning,"[9] Brad recalled years later as he reflected on his boisterous college years.

Brad thoroughly enjoyed college, polishing his charm while stretching his creativity. He wanted to use new ideas in his advertising classes, and at least one instructor appreciated his unusual thoughts. "I encourage my students to break the rules, but many of them are afraid to do that," said Birgit Wassmuth, one of Brad's college professors. "Brad took risks, though, because he's a highly creative person."[10]

A Man of Missou

Brad felt comfortable taking chances. He also had charisma and knew how to use it to his advantage. He posed shirtless for a "Men of Missou" charity fund-raising calendar and effortlessly attracted attention with his good looks.

"Brad was quite the flirt," said Michelle Burke, a classmate of Brad's at the University of Missouri. "It was a cutie-pie kind of flirt. A lot of my friends had big crushes on him, and he was so nice that most of them actually thought they had a shot with him.

"When he asked to borrow my notes before the final, naturally, I said yes. A few days later, a bouquet of carnations arrived at the sorority house where I lived. Written on the card was, 'Thanks for the notes—Brad.'"[11]

Nothing Serious

While Brad effortlessly attracted the attention of women on campus, he was having too much fun with his buddies to think of entering into a serious relationship. Brad was a member of the Sigma Chi fraternity and had a blast living with his friends in the frat house. Life with his friends was nothing like the strict Baptist upbringing Brad had experienced, and he began to distance himself from his churchgoing roots. He savored the freedom he had in the fraternity house, a place where the lifestyles of the residents sometimes imitated the antics of the misfits in the movie *Animal House.* The fun times Brad had there were the highlights of his college years. He sometimes had too much fun, however, arriving late to class and getting in just enough trouble to make things interesting.

The good times couldn't go on forever, however, and after four years of college, Brad realized he had outgrown frat house behavior. During his last semester, Brad found that he wouldn't be able to graduate as he expected. He was two credits short of fulfilling the college's requirements for a degree. He could complete

In college Pitt enjoyed living in a fraternity house, where the behavior of the residents at times resembled the crazy antics of the characters in the movie Animal House *(pictured).*

an independent study project that would give him the necessary credits and allow him to graduate on time, but as he thought about it, Brad wasn't certain he really wanted a career in advertising after all.

Heading for Hollywood

In college Brad had learned a lot from being on his own and discovered that he didn't want to settle into a career at an ad agency. As he pondered life after college, Brad made a decision. In his mind, he was done with college. Rather than finishing a final project that would have given him the credits he needed to graduate, he pointed his life in a new direction. "I decided everyone was applying for a job or getting married, and I didn't want to do either," [12] Brad said.

Brad had dreams that couldn't be realized in Missouri. Although his acting experience in college had been limited to skits in his fraternity's "Spring Fling" shows, two weeks before the end of the school year, he decided to take a risk. He realized he didn't need to

Although he was only two credits shy of a degree, Pitt decided to leave college and try his luck in Hollywood.

stay in his home state, that he could very easily head to California and see what it had to offer him.

In college Brad had found that he liked being independent and determining the path he would follow. He didn't want to be held back by commitments to a regular job or family. He wanted the chance to find success and happiness on his own terms.

Brad had grown up in a stable, religious family in the Midwest. His childhood and young adulthood gave him a solid foundation and the self-confidence to take chances. While he was happy in Missouri, he couldn't suppress a desire to see what else the world had to offer. When he decided to leave Missouri, he took with him a solid set of morals. His parents had nurtured this solid foundation and had given him a strong belief in himself. He had a set of standards to adhere to as he set off into the unknown.

The accolades he had received for his physical appearance, from adoring female classmates and the popularity of the "Men of Missou" calendar, and his childhood love of movies propelled him to try his luck in Hollywood. He was self-confident enough, and naive enough, to believe things would fall into place for him.

Brad was curious and restless, eager to see what awaited him as he left Missouri. The trips he made with his trucker father as a child awoke in him an early desire to see the world beyond the limits of his home state. The fun he had in college showed him that he enjoyed life the most when he was in the driver's seat. Now he was headed for a new world, filled with opportunity, challenge, disappointment, and success.

Chapter 2

Midwestern Kid in Hollywood

AS BRAD PITT drove toward Hollywood in the battered Nissan he called Runaround Sue, he didn't know what awaited him at the end of the road. But he knew that he couldn't rest until he found out. He was leaving behind the security of college life and the prospect of a stable job for the chance to experience excitement and glamour. Once he was on the road, he realized leaving was the right decision. He was relieved to be rid of the pressure of looking for a job he didn't really want. He was leaving college to pursue his dream, and his excitement grew as he passed each state line.

Pitt didn't want his family and friends to worry about him as he headed west to try his luck at an uncertain career, so he told them he would be attending the Art Center College of Design in Pasadena, California. The choice reflected his interest in drawing, and it would have made sense for him to go to school there. But he never really intended to take classes at the art center. He just dropped the name of the school as a ploy to keep people from being burdened with undue concerns about him. "They would just have thought I was crazy if I'd told them I wanted to be an actor," Pitt said. "People just don't think of being an actor in Springfield, Missouri. At least, not sane people." [13]

However, Pitt didn't fool his family for long. He landed an acting job several months after leaving Missouri and admitted to his parents that an acting career had been his real reason for heading west. They already suspected this might be the case. His dad had thought his son might try something daring. His mother wasn't sur-

26

prised because Pitt had always liked to try new things, and this career choice fit perfectly with his personality.

His friends from college were a bit more taken aback. They hadn't known the real reason he had headed west, and some were shocked to see him on an episode of the television comedy *Growing Pains.* Once the news sunk in, however, they could see that his new career choice suited him. He had a way with people that lent itself to a career in front of the camera. "People at Missouri were really surprised when they found out what Brad was doing," said Schudy, his college buddy. "But he's always been so charming that it made some sense." [14]

Taking Odd Jobs

Pitt didn't step in front of a camera the moment he entered Hollywood, however. Before he could impress his family and friends with his acting credentials, he had to break into the business.

Within months after leaving Missouri, Pitt landed a role on an episode of the popular television comedy, Growing Pains.

He arrived with $325 in his pocket and had to find a way to support himself.

Pitt spent his first few months in California taking whatever work he could find. He delivered refrigerators and collected money for the policemen's ball. The closest he came to acting was when he put on a giant chicken costume and made clucking sounds in front of an El Pollo Loco restaurant, trying to lure customers to the fast-food franchise. He didn't mind, however, because he was driven by the excitement of pursuing an acting career.

His next job was as a chauffeur, driving strippers to work in a limousine. He drove them to "strip-o-gram" jobs, collected the money, and drove them back. His respect for women gave him an instant dislike for this job, which showed him the darker side of Hollywood. He called it the worst job he ever had and felt sorry for the small-town girls who were trying to make it as actresses but were working as strippers instead.

Pitt hated the job and quit after three months. After he decided to give it up, he was persuaded to work for one more day. It was fortunate that he did. A stripper he chauffeured gave him the name of Roy London, an acting coach. Pitt found him to be an excellent teacher, just the person he needed to meet at that point in his career.

Pitt's odd jobs weren't exactly propelling him to stardom, but they gave him enough money to get by and the time to take acting classes. Pitt didn't look the part of a sexy Hollywood superstar while he was in London's class, but he had a special quality that set him apart from his classmates. In class students had to demonstrate their emotions in different situations. In one scene Pitt played a shy young man on a picnic with a woman he liked. He naturally knew how to carry off the scene. "He was standing up offering her some wine and twisting the stems in a very sexual manner," said his instructor, Ivana Chubbuck. "It was all subconscious. He was very unaware of what he had done and, when I told him, he just blushed." [15]

Pitt's female classmates also noticed how well he carried off the romantic scenes, but he didn't use the class to improve his social life. Instead, he concentrated on learning to act, preferring to stay at home and work on a scene rather than go to parties. Although the women in his class often gave him their attention, Pitt played the part of a loner.

In 1987 Pitt appeared in five episodes of the prime time soap opera
Dallas *as the love interest of actress Shalane McCall.*

Pitt's hard work in the class paid off. When a girl in the class
needed a scene partner in an audition for an agent, she asked Pitt
to help. He gladly obliged. The audition didn't end the way the girl
had hoped it would, however. In a turn of events that sounds almost as scripted as a Hollywood movie, Pitt was signed by the
agent instead.

Small Acting Roles

After a few months, Pitt found small acting jobs. He got a job as an
extra, standing in a doorway, in the movie *Less Than Zero* and appeared on the daytime soap opera *Another World.* In 1987 he made
his debut on *Dallas* as Randy, the beau of Priscilla Presley's daughter on the show. He appeared in five episodes of the prime time
soap opera.

For several weeks Pitt was involved in a real-life romance as
well with actress Shalane McCall, who played his love interest on
Dallas. It was the first time one of his on-screen romances spilled

into real life, but not the last. Pitt fell in love easily. He was a bit shy, but women were drawn to him, perhaps because he was polite and sensitive. He didn't always have the cash to treat women as he thought they should be treated, so his agent would loan him money so he could buy gifts for his girlfriends.

Jitka Pohlodek met Pitt when she was eighteen and working at a rental car counter at Los Angeles International Airport. Pitt managed to find her home phone number and gave her a call, asking if they could go on a date. Pohlodek, an aspiring actress from Little Rock, agreed. Pitt took her to dinner and they saw the movie *Good Morning, Vietnam.*

"It was exactly the same the second time we went out. There was no kiss until the third date," said Pohlodek, whose relationship with Pitt lasted several months. "He was very proper and sweet." [16]

Making an Impression

Pitt's list of acting credentials grew as he got small parts on *21 Jump Street, Tales from the Crypt,* the television movie *A Stoning in Fulham County,* and the popular drama *Thirtysomething.* Pitt's name still wasn't well-known, but he was beginning to make an impression on people in Hollywood. "Brad walking into a room was more exciting than most actors doing a scene," [17] said producer Patrick Hasburgh, who cast Pitt in *21 Jump Street* in 1988.

Pitt wowed Tracey Gold when he appeared on *Growing Pains,* a top-rated comedy on ABC, in 1987. Gold, then seventeen, was a regular on the series, which featured the family foibles of a mom, dad, and their children. After seeing Pitt's picture, Gold insisted he be hired to appear in the episode that featured her first on-screen kiss. Pitt was a bit nervous as he kissed Gold in front of the cast, crew, and Gold's mother. To Gold's embarrassment, he took care to make sure the scene met with the approval of her mother before going ahead with the kiss.

Pitt continued his television appearances in 1988, when he played an irascible adolescent in an episode of *Head of the Class.* The high school comedy starred Robin Givens, who endured a stormy marriage to former heavyweight champion Mike Tyson during the late 1980s before they were divorced. She and Pitt clicked offscreen as well as in front of the cameras and began dating.

Among Pitt's series of relationships with costars, his association with Givens was perhaps his most dangerous. Six months after he and Givens began dating, Pitt showed up with wine and firewood for a cozy evening in front of the fire. He ended up meeting Givens's ex-husband. Tyson is known for being hot-tempered. It took some quick talking by Givens to spare Pitt the wrath of Tyson's jealousy. Pitt and Givens split up soon after the incident.

First Starring Role

Pitt's career headed for the big screen when he traveled to Yugoslavia in 1988 to make the movie *The Dark Side of the Sun.* It was his first starring role in a feature film, and he was paid $1,523 a week for the seven-week shoot. He played an American with a rare skin disease who searches for a cure in Eastern Europe.

Pitt finished filming the movie, but political turmoil in Yugoslavia prevented the project from being completed. Pitt's movie was in the editing stages during this tumultuous time, and as

Pitt's first feature film was The Dark Side of the Sun, *in which he played an American with a rare skin disorder.*

a result it practically disappeared for eight years. The movie resurfaced in late 1996, when producer Angelo Arandjelovic began shopping it around to distributors. By that time Pitt was a superstar whose career had moved far beyond the low-budget project.

Taking the Next Step

Pitt's good looks also led to modeling jobs. An advertisement for Levi's jeans helped him get the notice he needed to take the next step in his career. He had a small role in the film *Happy Together* and was in the teen-slasher movie *Cutting Class*. He later called *Cutting Class* awful, but one reviewer said he and costar Donovan Leitch did an effective job alternating as good and bad guys.

Pitt and Juliette Lewis in the 1990 TV movie Too Young to Die. *Despite their nine-year age difference, Pitt fell in love with Lewis.*

Jill Schoelen was also in *Cutting Class* with Pitt, and they began dating. Their relationship was several months old when Schoelen called Pitt in L.A. from Budapest, Hungary, where she was making a movie. She told him she was lonely. Ever the romantic, thoughtful beau, he spent $600 of his last $800 on a plane ticket so he could pay her a surprise visit. He arrived on the European set only to be told she'd fallen in love with someone else.

Keeping Busy on TV

Pitt didn't waste time brooding over his breakup with Schoelen. He was soon busy with acting jobs, and in 1990 made the television movie *The Image* and the short-lived television series *Glory Days*. Although he wasn't impressed by his work, his role in *Glory Days* did garner some press coverage. Based on a Bruce Springsteen song by the same title, the series suggested that for some people, life goes downhill after high school. In *People Weekly*, Pitt was described as "Willem Dafoe's younger, cuter brother."[18] The series tried to create some male bonding banter but instead was deemed "overwritten" by *People*, with poor comedy and a lack of chemistry among the characters. Pitt agreed that the series was nothing to brag about.

A Long-Term Relationship

Pitt realized that roles in sitcoms would never take his career where he wanted it to go. He appreciated the work but realized that movies were a better showcase for his talent.

His next project was a role in the 1990 TV movie *Too Young to Die*, which led Pitt to his first long-term Hollywood relationship. In the movie Pitt takes advantage of Juliette Lewis's character, a young teenage runaway, and gets her hooked on drugs, beats her, and forces her into prostitution. In real life, he fell for his sixteen-year-old costar and treated her with respect. Although he was nine years older than Lewis, Pitt felt that Lewis was more mature than her age suggested. He didn't let the age gap bother him, and they began sharing a flat in Los Angeles almost immediately after they were done making their film.

Pitt was in awe of her talent. Lewis, whose father is actor Geoffrey Lewis, made her movie debut in the 1988 film *My*

Stepmother Is an Alien. She was also in *National Lampoon's Christmas Vacation* and later earned an Academy Award nomination for her performance in *Cape Fear.* Pitt admired her range and powerful acting ability.

He and Lewis were in a cutthroat business but tried not to let professional competition slip into their personal lives. They talked over their problems before they were overwhelmed by them. It wasn't easy, but they tried to keep work separate from their relationship.

Getting a Break

Pitt paid his dues by working hard in small roles and low-budget projects. He was due for a break, and it came with his performance in Ridley Scott's *Thelma and Louise.* Pitt spent fifteen minutes on-screen in the 1991 film as the sexy hitchhiker who woos and robs Thelma, played by Geena Davis. His portrayal of the smooth-talking J. D. earned him instant fame as he heated up the screen.

Pitt wasn't the director's first choice for the role, however. It was only after actor William Baldwin left the film to star in the movie *Backdraft* that Pitt was called in to read with Davis. Sparks flew between the pair, and it was clear that Pitt was the right choice.

Pitt was shy and nervous while filming the famous love scene with Davis. He was concerned his mother wouldn't approve of the steamy scene, but at the same time knew it was the type of role that could make his career. "I figured it would be a role like J. D.— something I'm good at, a Southern guy—that would make the break," Pitt said. "It basically opened the door for some kind of respect, working with all those great people." [19]

The role was the closest Pitt had come to playing himself to that point in his career. Although he has candidly said that making the scene was far from romantic, his natural charisma and charm effortlessly came through on the screen. He was a star from the moment he appeared in *Thelma and Louise.*

Pitt's scene with Davis was so hot that there were rumors that Pitt got cozy offscreen with her as well. However, his relationship with Lewis continued and gave Pitt his first taste of life in the public

Thelma and Louise

Thelma and Louise was an important movie for reasons other than being Brad Pitt's first taste of stardom. The movie portrayed two female characters on the road in the style of a buddy movie, a genre typically dominated by men. Susan Sarandon and Geena Davis play best friends who are on the run from the law and heading toward the unknown.

Davis's character, Thelma Dickson, is a housewife who is tired of her chauvinistic husband and her life as a submissive homemaker. Sarandon's Louise Sawyer is frustrated by her boyfriend's inability to commit to a relationship. They embark on a road trip that turns out to be one mistake after another but is empowering nonetheless.

The misadventures begin when Louise shoots a would-be rapist. She and Thelma head toward Mexico, meeting Pitt's J. D. along the way. He teaches them how to politely commit robbery and proceeds to steal their money, after a famous interlude with Thelma. Thelma and Louise continue their trek, outwitting the police along the way and leading them to a memorable showdown at the edge of the Grand Canyon.

The movie's less-than-complimentary portrayal of male characters had some critics calling the film degrading to men. It was also criticized for being violent and angry. However, the film did well at the box office and won an Oscar for Best Original Screenplay. Its stars supported the movie, saying that the outcry stemmed from the fact that the violence was directed at men by women and that the same type of scrutiny was not given to films that centered on male-on-female violence.

Susan Sarandon and Geena Davis are two friends running from the law in the 1991 film Thelma and Louise.

Pitt's brief but sexy role in Thelma and Louise *showcased his natural charisma and earned him instant fame.*

eye. They attracted attention as a hot Hollywood couple, and reporters from the *National Enquirer* even went through their trash.

Their careers put them in the spotlight as well, although Lewis's star was shining much brighter than Pitt's. In 1992 she made the movie *Cape Fear,* and he stood on the sidelines as the spotlight focused on her at the movie's premiere. He was relaxing, waiting for her to finish promoting the film, when a TV crew flashed their lights his way and asked if he would answer a few questions. Pitt agreed, and a voice asked, "How does it feel to be on *Beverly Hills, 90210?*"

"I'm not on *90210,*" Pitt said with a laugh. Immediately, the lights dimmed. Pitt was more amused than upset. "Just like that," Pitt said. "Fade to black. I got a kick out of that."[20]

Pitt might not have been universally known at that time, but his role in *Thelma and Louise* had dramatically changed his life. He had come to California as a naive midwesterner and five years later was on his way to stardom. He quickly learned about the struggling life of a young actor, but his odd jobs in a chicken suit and as a limo driver only served to inspire him to work harder. The work ethic he learned from his family served him well, and he soon landed small TV roles before catching his big break with *Thelma and Louise.* His next challenge was to hang on to the inner qualities that had helped him get to this point and not let them get lost in the swirl of stardom.

Chapter 3

In Charge

Pitt was offered many roles after his widely acclaimed but brief appearance in *Thelma and Louise* but rejected the parts that called on him to play only good-looking, empty characters. He could have made a career out of playing characters similar to J. D., but the same independent nature that drove him to leave Missouri for California prevented him from capitulating to Hollywood stereotypes.

Brad wanted to avoid being labeled as the next James Dean, the next Robert Redford, or the next Tom Cruise, and he worked hard to carve his own niche in Hollywood. He had some leverage in deciding which roles to accept, and he used it to his advantage. Instead of being a standard Hollywood heartthrob, Pitt directed his career to avoid roles that called for a mindless but handsome hero.

Showing His Versatility

Pitt presented a variety of images between 1989 and 1992 when he made the movies *Across the Tracks, The Favor, Johnny Suede,* and *Cool World.* The roles took him from playing an artist in spectacles to a pompadour-coiffed teen idol to a cartoon cop, as he broadened his horizons with a series of challenging roles.

Across the Tracks paired Pitt with Rick Schroder, who was in the midst of making a career transition from child star to adult actor. They play brothers with very different personalities who alternately save each other from making major mistakes in their lives. Pitt received praise for his role in the average movie. "The film's strength lies in the two leads, and particularly the depiction of straight-arrow Joe (played by Pitt), whose virtue and discipline

38

mask an obsessed, fragile personality," wrote Jay Robert Nash in the 1992 edition of *The Motion Picture Guide.* "He could develop into a major player."[21]

Pitt also had a supporting role in *The Favor*, which was made in 1991 but released in 1994 because of its producer's financial difficulties. Pitt plays the artist boyfriend of Elizabeth McGovern's character, who is asked to do a favor for her best friend. The friend, a housewife given to daydreaming, wants McGovern to romance her handsome high school sweetheart because she can't stop fantasizing about him. The rather complicated plot yields a bland movie.

Pitt and Rick Schroder in Across the Tracks. *Pitt received favorable reviews for his acting, but the film did not do well.*

In the low-budget comedy *Johnny Suede*, Pitt lifted his hair into a pompadour, playing a would-be teen idol. He got the job before receiving acclaim for his role in *Thelma and Louise* and took it because he wanted to keep his work interesting. One reviewer said Pitt's performance was the only thing that made the film watchable.

Live action and animation are mixed in *Cool World*, where Pitt plays a police officer in a parallel cartoon universe. Although the movie was cast before Pitt's *Thelma and Louise* fame, he won the *Cool World* part over two hundred actors. "Brad walked in the room, did a reading and blew me away," said Ralph Bakshi, who directed the film. "I thought he was the only one who could do this part."[22]

The film makes wide use of a blue-screen technique that allows actors to play opposite cartoon characters. It came four years after the technically acclaimed *Who Framed Roger Rabbit?* and was

Pitt sported a pompadour for the 1992 low-budget comedy Johnny Suede.

Making *Cool World*

Cool World was made with a filming technique that uses blue screens to combine live action and animation. To achieve this special effect, live actors are filmed in front of a blue screen. The blue area is filled in later with computer-generated special effects or animation.

Blue screens are used in the movies to add special effects to a film and are also commonly used by television weather forecasters. The weather forecaster appears to be standing in front of a map but is really standing in front of a blue screen. The weather map is superimposed over the screen.

Acting with characters who are to be added later is not easy. Pitt disliked reacting to invisible characters while shooting *Cool World*. "If you have an ego, you'll lose it, just having to do this with all these people standing around," Pitt said, pretending to kiss an invisible girl. "That'll humble you real quickly."

Pitt's role in Cool World *required him to act opposite cartoon characters that were drawn in after filming.*

criticized for ineptly blending animation and live acting. Pitt found it difficult to act opposite characters who were drawn in after he was done filming his lines, and his performance was called uncomfortable.

However, Pitt's decision to take on challenging roles helped rather than hurt his career. Even if he didn't pull off every role

Pitt (left) jumped at the opportunity to work with director Robert Redford (right) on the film A River Runs Through It.

perfectly, he was given credit for stretching his talent. By trying new things, he was proving he was capable of more than looking good on the screen. He could have been satisfied with being a teen idol but showed he was a serious actor by choosing interesting and difficult parts.

Working with Redford

Pitt didn't let the lukewarm reviews for *Cool World* get him down. Instead, he set his sights on a loftier project. Robert Redford, a much-acclaimed actor and director, was planning to make a movie based on the novella *A River Runs Through It* by Norman Maclean. The book tells of fishing and family relationships and intrigued Pitt, who appreciated films that showed a man standing up for his principles. The role of Paul Maclean—the book's doomed, rough-and-tumble, ace fly fisherman—was sought by many top actors. Pitt wasn't intimidated by the competition, however. He did everything he could to win the job.

When he heard Redford was going to make the movie, Pitt immediately read Maclean's book. He thought the book was beautiful, and it touched his heart. He began thinking about the character a year before the movie was made and kept a close eye on the progress of the project. When it came time for him to audition in front of Redford, he found himself in front of a man with a powerful presence. The audition was challenging and Pitt had high expectations for himself. However, after it was over he wasn't happy with his performance.

Pitt asked for another chance. At home he redid his two *River* audition scenes on tape. He got help from his *Johnny Suede* costar Catherine Keener, who made period costumes for the scenes, and her husband, Dermot Mulroney, who helped turn the scenes into a feature. Melissa Etheridge, a musician and another of Pitt's friends, provided background music.

However, it was what Pitt said and did in Redford's office rather than how he acted on the tape that impressed Redford. "Brad had an inner conflict that was very interesting to me," Redford said. "He's an extremely smart guy inside, quite sensitive, but it's all covered over with the part that needs to act tough to get along in the world."[23]

Pitt worked hard to live up to the director's expectations. His first job was to learn proper fly-fishing techniques, since his character is an expert at the sport. Fly-fishing involves casting with a precise rhythm, and it wasn't easy for Pitt to find open areas in

crowded Los Angeles where he could work on his technique. He ended up practicing on top of buildings in Hollywood before he left to film the movie in Montana. This wasn't without mishap, as Pitt would routinely hook himself in the back of the head.

Pitt loved making *River* on location in Montana. A country boy at heart, he

Pitt's first challenge for his role in A River Runs Through It *was learning proper fly-fishing techniques.*

rented a house and brought his coon dog Deacon with him. He could be at ease there, in contrast to the more watchful and wary demeanor he had to display in Los Angeles.

Gaining Valuable Experience

Pitt was still a rather young and inexperienced actor when he made *River*, and Redford had to work with him to get the performance he wanted. Redford molded Pitt into the character of Paul, the rebellious, self-destructive minister's son. He coached him to play the part of a vibrant, demonstrative individual who was very comfortable with himself.

Pitt said Redford taught him how to act gracefully and how to powerfully convey emotions and thoughts without words. Through Redford's tutoring, Pitt was able to show the complicated inner workings of his character. He was able to transcend his own good looks and let the character's complex personality come through.

Pitt, however, knew where he wanted to draw the line when getting into character for a role. He didn't believe in excessive preparation and analysis. Instead, he acted on instinct and impulse, only completely understanding his character when he saw the finished movie.

Pitt achieved the right balance in *River*, and the movie showed that Pitt had "it," that mystical quality of which stars are made. Although he was still green and insecure while making *River*, his charisma effortlessly comes through. His costar Tom Skerritt could tell that Pitt was at the beginning of a very successful career. "You could see that he was going to be one of those that they would choose—and the Powers That Be always seem to choose who's going to be the heir apparent," said Skerritt, who played Pitt's father in *River*. "Redford was that. Cruise was that. Now Pitt."[24]

Much was made of the resemblance between Pitt and Redford, to Pitt's great chagrin. One critic said Pitt dyed his hair blond for the role, which he denied. Pitt and Redford said their similar good looks were only a coincidence.

Getting Good Reviews

Pitt's performance in *River* impressed critics. He got good reviews for his looks and charm, and the poetic, nostalgic story was well

Although Pitt did not think it was one of his best performances, critics praised him for his work in A River Runs Through It.

received. Pitt was a little surprised at how well the movie did. He had felt pressure while making the film and thought it was one of his weaker performances.

Despite Pitt's reservations about his performance, Pitt's role in *River* added fuel to his already hot career. As his success began to sink in, he was wary. He knew he had to be careful taking his next steps. His dreams were coming true, but it was happening so quickly that he was overwhelmed. He relied on his strong character to help him maintain a sense of stability.

Career Decisions

Pitt needed some space after making *River*. He spent two and a half months living overseas after filming was completed. He used the time abroad to think about where he wanted to take his career. He needed to decide if he could continue acting without losing his integrity.

Pitt admitted that he wasn't always the most practical guy. Rather, he often acted to suit his needs of the moment. Sometimes he just needed to feel like he was free to act on impulse.

"I'm very impractical," he said. "I couldn't tell you the price of gas—all I know is, I need gas. I like to drive on a hot day with my windows down and the air conditioner on. Just feels good.

"They say when a dog sticks his head out a car window, it puts him in a state of constant euphoria," Pitt said, leaning out a car window while with a reporter. "I can understand."[25]

Taking His Time

Pitt spent almost a year after *River* reading scripts but was in no hurry to take an acting job. In early 1992 the twenty-eight-year-old Pitt shared a three-bedroom house in West Hollywood with actor Buck Simmons, whom he had met while making *River*. He didn't mind doing mundane home improvement projects. He had visions for the yard, including a croquet court in the front, an archery range along the side, and a basketball court in the driveway. He slept on a foam pad on the floor of his closet, because the sun glared through the windows and was too bright for him. The room was almost empty, except for a few boxes. It was here that Pitt contemplated the next moves in his career. He wanted to find a role that was special.

Pitt saw acting as an art rather than a business, but along with his fame came advice that he didn't always want to hear. People told him that now, since he was worth so much, he had something to lose if he made a bad decision. He tried hard to keep a cool head and not be driven by fear of failure.

Downplaying His Good Looks

When Pitt decided on his next career move, it was again in a direction that played down his good looks. In 1993 he took a small part in the movie *True Romance*, playing a spaced-out druggie. He wasn't interested in playing a typical hero, instead taking a minor role in the film.

His next project was the crime drama *Kalifornia* with his girlfriend Juliette Lewis. Pitt overcame his good looks to play a scruffy character, gaining twenty pounds and sporting a greasy beard and

Pitt's Changing Looks

Brad Pitt loves to toy with his handsome image and play with his good looks. He adopted a clean-cut beach-boy look when he first came to Hollywood but sported a grungy, seedy facade by the time he was named the Sexiest Man Alive in 1995.

A 1988 publicity photo shows off his well-toned arms, abdominal muscles, and tanned skin. Looking into the camera with pouting lips and a questioning gaze, his hair flips restlessly over the side of a white bandanna, leaving his left ear exposed to show a dangling cross-shaped earring.

After achieving success, Pitt was so intent on being recognized as an actor rather than a pretty face that he deliberately downplayed his looks offscreen, sporting a beard and often dressing in grunge fashions. He let his blond hair grow long and tangled and sometimes hid it beneath a knit cap. On the cover of *People Weekly* after being named the Sexiest Man Alive, he gazed intently at the camera with a more self-assured look than he showed in the early publicity shot. His hair may be askew, but the irresistible nature of his crisp blue eyes can't be denied.

During his relationship with Gwyneth Paltrow, Pitt reverted to a more clean-cut image, with shorter hair and a clean-shaven face. He settled on a semiscruffy but handsome look after their breakup, with a goatee and a haircut above his ears. When he was named the Sexiest Man Alive in 2000, *People Weekly*'s cover shot shows Pitt with tousled hair, the same steely blue eyes, and just the hint of a smile above a chin bristling with razor stubble. Having firmly asserted himself as his own man, he was free to let his good looks shine through in his own down-home manner.

Regardless of whether he is sporting a clean-cut or a grunge look, Pitt's natural good looks always shine through.

hair for the role of creepy serial killer Early Grayce. However, director Dominic Sena claimed Pitt still made the women on the set swoon.

Pitt's character has few redeeming qualities, and critics found the character and the film very hard to like. One critic praised Pitt's acting as full-bodied, but another, who gave the film a D rating, said, "There's nothing to experience in *Kalifornia* besides a mountain of ostentatious bad acting. Pitt and Lewis are straining for downscale Method seriousness, but with their strenuous *Hee Haw* accents, both of the gifted young actors come off as embarrassingly mannered."[26]

Pitt and Lewis in the gritty 1993 film Kalifornia. *Pitt gained twenty pounds and grew a full beard to play the role of the creepy serial killer Early Grayce.*

The difficulties of having a public relationship took their toll and Pitt and Lewis broke up shortly after filming Kalifornia.

The relationship between Pitt and Lewis was strained offscreen as well. Although it looked like their three-year relationship was on solid ground when they made the movie together, they broke up soon after filming ended. They had tried to keep career and ego from hurting their relationship, but Pitt's growing popularity may have doomed things for the couple. Lewis later said that it was difficult to have a public relationship with Pitt.

Two years later Pitt said he still loved Lewis. He appreciated her originality and quirks, such as her unusual fashion decision to wear cornrows to the Oscars. But he was wise enough to know that it takes more than love to sustain a relationship. "The problem is, we grow up with this vision that love conquers all, and that's just not so, is it?"[27] Pitt said.

Pitt knew he didn't have all the answers when it came to his personal or professional life. His brief appearance in *Thelma and Louise* brought him the fame he had come to Hollywood to acquire. Once he had it, he learned that it didn't make his life any easier. He took time to analyze his career and his life, thinking about where he wanted to go without compromising his integrity or the charming personality that made him so appealing.

Chapter 4

Success

PITT WAS ON the verge of becoming a superstar in mid-1993. Already famous, he was about to take things to a new level. He challenged himself, made choices with confidence, and didn't look back. When things didn't turn out as he expected, he learned from the experience and moved on to his next project.

After venturing into new territory with *Kalifornia* and *True Romance*, Pitt returned to playing the romantic role it seemed his chiseled body was made for in the Western *Legends of the Fall*. He spent a rainy summer in 1993 in Calgary, Alberta, Canada, filming the story about the three sons of a retired cavalry officer who fall in

Pitt felt he was well-suited for the romantic role of the wild, rebellious Tristan in the epic Legends of the Fall.

love with the same woman. Pitt liked the wild, rebellious nature of Tristan, the untamed son, and said the role fit his personality.

Pitt was chosen for the role in part because of the impression he made on *Legends* director Ed Zwick and producer Marshall Herskovitz when he had a one-line guest appearance on *Thirtysomething* in 1989. They had created the drama, and Pitt's appearance on the show stuck in Herskovitz's memory. "He caused such a stir on the set," Herskovitz said. "He was so good-looking and so charismatic and such a sweet guy, everybody knew he was going places." [28]

Women loved the romantic aspect of *Legends*. Pitt, with sexy, flowing long hair, showed star presence as he captured the untamed spirit of his character. "Pitt is both credible and compelling," [29] one critic wrote. Pitt was compared to the legendary James Dean for his appearance, style, talent, and charisma. He was at ease and comfortable in front of the camera, and his self-confidence showed up on the screen.

Pitt's performance wasn't universally loved, however, and the film was at times an engaging epic and at others a drawn-out bore. One critic wrote, "As the most troubled of the trio, Pitt is front and center, with mixed results. Sometimes his portrayal of a man at war with himself is moving; at other times he seems to be all attitude, like the models in Calvin Klein underwear ads." [30]

A Major Challenge

After filming *Legends*, Pitt immediately moved onto his next project. He spent five months in New Orleans and Paris making *Interview with the Vampire* with Tom Cruise. The role of Louis de Pointe du Lac was extremely challenging, almost agonizing, for Pitt as he played a depressed widower lured into the world of the undead by Cruise's character, Lestat. Throughout the movie, Pitt's character wants to kill himself. Pitt had never considered taking his own life, and the thought sickened him. He didn't like the way the role got into his subconscious and ruined his mood every day.

Other problems resulted from a clash of acting styles between Pitt and Cruise. Cruise's methodical, precise style contrasted sharply with Pitt's laid-back, hang-loose attitude. Differences between the characters they played also affected their relationship on

Pitt had a difficult time filming Interview with the Vampire. *The dark, depressing role affected his mood and he clashed with his costar Tom Cruise.*

the set. Cruise's Lestat loved to control the situation and create pain for Pitt's character, who wanted to escape. The actors often related to each other on the set the way their characters did in the film. Pitt, already tired from making *Legends*, agonized over his performance and relationship with his costar.

There was also an underlying competition between the stars that got in the way of any real conversations and stifled any camaraderie that might have evolved. Cruise reportedly wore lifts in his shoes so he could be nearer to the height of his six-foot costar. Other troubles included criticism from author Anne Rice, who complained about the casting. She said the selections of Cruise and Pitt were "like casting Huck Finn and Tom Sawyer." [31]

However, by the time the film was finished, Rice recanted her negative statements and put her full support behind the project. Pitt said that he was very impressed by Cruise's performance and that what looked like tension on the set was the result of Pitt's drifting lifestyle contrasting with Cruise's controlled one. He said he liked Cruise and took responsibility for any resentment he felt during filming, saying it stemmed from the characters they were playing.

Once filming was completed, Pitt was ready to forget how serious everything seemed while they were making the movie.

Good Reviews

However difficult it was for Pitt to make *Vampire,* in it he accomplished his goal of playing against his image. His dark performance as the grim and disturbed Louis wouldn't be confused with the adventuresome Tristan he played in *Legends of the Fall.* He was lauded for his talent and good looks and called one of the brightest stars in Hollywood.

Vampire was a success and true to the novel it was based on, but it was criticized for some holes in the plot and some of its more ghoulish aspects. The inner turmoil Pitt felt while making the film translated to a well-received adaptation of his character on the screen. "Cruise works hard, has some good moments, but too many fissures appear in the portrait," wrote one critic. "Brad Pitt, more lithe than Cruise and more adept at suggesting morbidity and inner solitude, comes closer to success as Louis." [32]

While making the movie, Pitt yearned to have a little of the privacy he enjoyed in the days before he was a star. He tired of having his every move monitored. He didn't want fans to know everything about him and dreaded becoming a hollow Hollywood personality.

Relaxing at Home

Pitt's personality was too engaging for people to leave him alone. He was a star and paid the price through public interest in his day-to-day life. However, he also enjoyed the trappings of

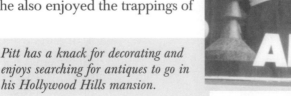

Pitt has a knack for decorating and enjoys searching for antiques to go in his Hollywood Hills mansion.

Pitt's Home and Penchant for Decorating

Brad Pitt has an eye for style and a penchant for decorating his thirty-one-room mansion. He is constantly thinking about remodeling the early-twentieth-century home and is especially keen on proportion, materials, light, and perspective. The home represents Pitt's idealism and quest for perfection and may never be finished.

The multiterraced home is meticulously decorated to suit his tastes with old leather sofas, green rockers on the front porch, and Arts and Crafts furnishings. "He's got really good taste," said his friend Paul Feldsher. "Pitt has an unbelievable eye. We can walk into a store together and he'll see the tiniest thing that anyone might have missed, and he'll nail it right away. That's something you would not expect of a macho, vapid movie star." Pitt chronicled the five-year restoration of his home in a photo essay included in the book *Greene & Greene: The Blacker House*, a book about the Arts and Crafts movement by architects Randell L. Makinson and Thomas A. Heinz.

Pitt constantly feeds his interest in architecture. While on the set of several movies, Pitt passed his free time by indulging in his interest. During production delays for *The Devil's Own*, Pitt stayed in his trailer and toyed with architectural plans. While making *Interview with the Vampire*, Pitt took a side trip to Glasgow, sketch pad in hand, to study the architecture of Charles Rennie Mackintosh.

Pitt loves drawing as well as architecture, sketching everything from chairs to cities. When he's in chaotic relationships, he leans toward the linear, proportioned Frank Lloyd Wright type of drawing. But when he's in a more stable relationship, he leans toward the whimsical and free-flowing.

success in his early-twentieth-century mansion that he filled with antiques.

After making *Vampire*, Pitt headed home to relax. Two months after breaking up with Lewis, Pitt rekindled his romance with the soft-spoken Pohlodek. They lived in his stunning Hollywood Hills home, formerly owned by Elvira, Mistress of the Dark. Along with the antique tables and Tiffany lamps Pitt had carefully selected, also on display in the thirty-one-room home was the shotgun his father gave him, alongside a twelve-gauge and a handgun, a reminder of his Missouri upbringing. Their pets—an assortment of dogs, chameleons, and iguanas, along with a pair of bobcats—inhabited the grounds. Pitt tried to lead a rather normal life, hanging out at home with his girlfriend, playing with their pets, and watching television.

Taking a look at his elegant surroundings, Pitt realized that he had made significant strides in his career. However, he also knew that if he wanted his career to be a long one, he couldn't rest on his success. He had to continue to find roles to propel his career while not becoming overly impressed with his own achievements. He knew his thriving career could come to an abrupt end and tried to be honest with himself.

Sexiest Man Alive

At the end of 1994, Pitt wasn't certain where his career or life would take him. His romance with Pohlodek ended for good that year, and Pitt was critical of himself when he analyzed his ability as an actor. He felt he was a good and consistent actor with glimmers of greatness but knew he could also turn in a subpar performance.

By the following January, however, Pitt could have little doubt that his fame was cemented when he was named *People Weekly*'s Sexiest Man Alive. The magazine lauded him for being an enigma, a complex person whose boyish, vulnerable charm captivated women, yet who also worked hard in quirky roles and didn't always rely on his good looks to carry himself on-screen. He constantly renewed his image and was conscious of how he was guiding his life, not just his career.

Pitt was chosen as the Sexiest Man Alive partly because he was a puzzle, an unpretentious midwesterner who would sometimes hang out with rock star Kurt Cobain's widow, Courtney Love, at the Viper Room in L.A. He was equally comfortable holding a sketch pad or a twelve-guage in his hand. He had a classic American style that made him both likable and lovable.

Pitt wasn't impressed by the title, however, and didn't let the latest affirmation of his good looks go to his head. "A friend of mine said they misspelled it," Pitt said. "It was supposed to be sexiest moron." [33]

Pitt didn't want to be recognized for only his physical qualities and went to lengths to hide them with long hair and a grungy appearance in public. He wanted to be appealing as much for his inner soul as his handsome visage. He didn't let his star status affect the way he acted toward others. He was constantly trying to get beyond his good looks by burying his ego and being attentive to the needs of others.

Directing His Career

Pitt didn't revel in the title of Sexiest Man Alive. Rather, he continued to play against his good looks by taking on the role of a gritty homicide detective in the crime thriller *Seven*. In the unusual suspense movie, Pitt and costar Morgan Freeman track a killer whose attacks are based on the seven deadly sins. It was a project that Pitt welcomed. After doing his own stunts in *Legends* and making the emotionally draining *Vampire*, he was ready for a role that was less taxing physically and emotionally.

With *Seven*, Pitt showed he was adept at directing his career. He had been around long enough that his ability was no longer a surprise, so he had to offer more to keep people's interest. "It used to be about proving myself," he said. "Now, if I'm not careful, it can be about just holding on. I'm not going to let that happen. I'm looking for something different every time out." [34]

Pitt put his all into the role. One scene called for him to drop from a fire escape and run across several vehicles. During filming, he slipped and fell through the windshield of a car, injuring his arm.

In the suspense movie Seven, *Pitt and costar Morgan Freeman play homicide detectives who track a serial killer whose gruesome crimes are based on the seven deadly sins.*

Falling in Love Again

Much of the film had to be reshot because Pitt's arm was put into a cast after his accident. But more time on the set also meant that Pitt got to spend more time with the latest love of his life, Gwyneth Paltrow. Paltrow, who plays the role of Pitt's wife in the film, was an accomplished actress with a bright future. The twenty-two-year-old daughter of actress Blythe Danner and director Bruce Paltrow, she was as sophisticated as he was down-home. The pair soon realized that opposites do indeed attract. "I knew immediately," Pitt

Gwyneth Paltrow's Career

Gwyneth Kate Paltrow was born on September 28, 1972, in Los Angeles. Her family, no stranger to the entertainment business, moved to New York City when she was eleven. Dinner conversation often touched on her mother's stage roles and her father's television productions. Her mother appeared as Blanche DuBois in *A Streetcar Named Desire* and her father created the shows *The White Shadow* and *St. Elsewhere*.

Paltrow attended the elite Spence School, an academy for girls in Manhattan. After graduating she returned to the West Coast. She enrolled at the University of California at Santa Barbara, intending to study art history. She left college after realizing she was more committed to becoming an actress than to her studies. One of her first roles was alongside her mother in the Williamstown Theatre production of *Picnic*.

Her first film was the 1991 movie *Shout* with John Travolta. She also played the young Wendy in Steven Spielberg's *Hook*. She took other stage and screen roles, including *Flesh and Bone* in 1993 and of course *Seven* with Pitt in 1995. She won an Oscar for her performance in *Shakespeare in Love* in 1998. *Duets*, the film she and Pitt planned to make together before their split, was released in 2000, with Paltrow but not Pitt in the cast.

Gwyneth Paltrow gets a kiss from her father after winning the Oscar for Best Actress in Shakespeare in Love.

Pitt and Paltrow fell in love while shooting Seven, *in which she plays his wife.*

later said. "I got within 10 feet of her, and I got goofy. I couldn't talk." [35]

Paltrow was a little more hesitant, however, to admit she had feelings for Pitt. She fought the chemistry that was building between them. "I started getting a crush on him," she said. "I'm like, 'Are you sane? You can't get a crush on Brad Pitt. Get a hold of yourself.'" [36]

A Serious Romance

Soon, however, she gave in to her feelings. Pitt called Paltrow his "angel," and the pair began a serious romance. They shared a Greenwich Village apartment and frequented a bar called Hogs & Heifers in Manhattan. They held hands over dinner at the intimate Italian restaurant Villa Mosconi and embraced while standing in line waiting to grab a bite to eat late at night. Paltrow said her happiest day was spent with Pitt in a little coffee shop. "We woke up

late and were having a lazy morning, and we went around the corner and had these big bowls of latte and sat there all sleepy,"[37] she
said.

They seemed made for each other, with every moment together somehow intimately romantic. They felt comfortable in
each other's worlds. He attended a showing of her movie *Emma* at
the White House, and she danced on the bar at Hogs & Heifers.
Even their disagreements were cute. When Paltrow was comfortable, Pitt was too hot. Paltrow thought they stayed home too much;
Pitt thought they went out all the time.

Growing up with an actress for a mother and a director for a
father, Paltrow was much more savvy about show business than
Pitt. She taught him the danger of overexposure and helped him
exist under the bright lights. In turn, Pitt taught her that it was all
right just to hang out at home. They watched movies and ate dinner in their pajamas and just bummed around. Their personalities
balanced each other.

Pitt and Paltrow were favorites of the press, and every Monday
morning their publicists would fax them the latest tabloid articles
about them. They joked about it, reading through the tabloids to
see what they were supposedly doing.

When the pair went to Pitt's parents' home in December 1995
for the Christmas holidays, Pitt was noticed by fans at a local su-
permarket while picking up some groceries for the family.
Although Pitt wore a wool scarf and long dark coat, he was recognized immediately and asked to sign some autographs. Paltrow,
wearing high-top tennis shoes and a stocking cap, went largely un-
noticed and had a breathless checkout girl confide in her that Pitt
was in the store. Paltrow pretended not to know who he was, and
then laughed.

Although Paltrow was also an accomplished actress, she was
confident enough in her ability not to be threatened by the attention given to Pitt. She didn't mind being known as Brad Pitt's girlfriend and took her new title in stride. "If a housewife in Wisconsin
has to peg me as Brad Pitt's girlfriend, fine," Paltrow said. "I am his
girlfriend. But the people who make movies don't. I'm in a great
position now. I can choose the work I want, yet if I go out by myself to the mall, I don't get mobbed like Brad."[38]

Embarrassed by Photos

Sometimes their sought-after privacy was hard to come by, however. When the pair was vacationing in St. Bart's in the spring, a photographer snapped photos of them sunbathing in the nude. The photos first appeared in British tabloids, showed up on the Internet, and were eventually published in *Playgirl.* News of the photos surfaced on a morning the pair was set to have breakfast with Paltrow's father.

"Brad is an extremely private person," said Tom DiCillo, Pitt's friend who directed him in *Johnny Suede.* "In a certain way he's horrified. He can't comprehend that people would waste time doing that in the first place."[39]

Despite the embarrassment the photos caused, Paltrow's parents accepted Pitt. They weren't wild about their daughter dating a movie star at first, but after they met him they were as charmed by him as everyone else. They appreciated his integrity, his lack of vanity, and the depth of his personality.

Getting Better

Pitt and Paltrow did well on-screen as well. *Seven,* although downbeat and edgy, was an astounding success due to the ability of Pitt to draw moviegoers to the box office. In the movie Pitt plays a gritty young detective, while Freeman is a sage nearing retirement. Pitt brought energy to his role.

Audio Books

Brad Pitt's respect for the American West comes through in his reading of Cormac McCarthy's Border Trilogy. In a soft southern drawl reminiscent of his roles in *Legends of the Fall* and *A River Runs Through It,* Pitt narrates the three volumes that bring to life characters such as John Grady Cole and Billy Parham. The three-volume collection includes *All the Pretty Horses, The Crossing,* and *Cities of the Plain.*

The trilogy, which won the National Book Award in 1992, recreates the West as it was when the old ways were fading. Pitt reads an abridged version, which does not include some longer, philosophical passages and some Spanish passages. Pitt is a longtime admirer of McCarthy's literary style and enjoyed reading his earlier novel *Blood Meridian* in addition to narrating the Border books.

Seven earned Pitt the best praise of his career to date and, at $8 million, his biggest paycheck to that point. Although he had been in the spotlight for years, his success and the riches that came with it still felt a little strange to him. He had been happy when he had nothing and knew that if everything he had evaporated, he would still be able to get along all right.

Pitt again wanted to do something different after *Seven* and faced the challenge of choosing the right project. Life was easier when he had to take any job he could get, he said. Now that he had the opportunity to choose, there was pressure to pick a winner. He thought about doing something new, perhaps a comedy, but was particular about the script. He also thought about taking on a role so different that audiences wouldn't even recognize him.

Pitt found what he was looking for in the role of an unbalanced animal activist in the quirky science fiction adventure film *12 Monkeys*, directed by Terry Gilliam. He had a supporting role in the futuristic drama, backing up stars Bruce Willis and Madeleine Stowe. Set in the year 2035, the movie has Willis playing a pris-

Pitt won a Golden Globe and an Oscar nomination for his role as a psychotic mental patient in 12 Monkeys.

oner sent back in time from an underground society to find the source of a virus that wiped out most of humankind in the year 1997. He ends up in a mental institution, where he meets Pitt, who uses wild hand gestures and tics to emphasize his character's odd personality. Pitt wore brown cross-eyed contact lenses over his baby blues and twisted his mouth into a psychotic grin as he tried to make himself less attractive in the film. However, the change in eye color wasn't enough to mask his good looks.

Taking a supporting role as a psychotic character in the futuristic film was another way for Pitt to stretch his ability. To prepare for the role, he went to group therapy sessions in a Philadelphia hospital for two weeks and checked into a psychiatric ward for a day. Paltrow, who was getting ready to shoot the films *The Pallbearer* and *Emma*, kept him grounded. "He was fully in character. He is a perfectionist," said Charles Roven, the producer of *12 Monkeys*. "She keeps him straight and aware of reality." [40]

After being the featured attraction in *Seven*, it may have seemed like a step backward for Pitt to take a supporting role in a film. Although his role in *12 Monkeys* was atypical star behavior, it shows that Pitt likes to surprise audiences. Throughout his career, Pitt has liked to make interesting choices.

Again Pitt's choice of the role and hard work paid off. He won a Golden Globe Award and earned an Oscar nomination for his hyperactive role. He was still critical of his performance, however, and said he thought he could have done a better job if he had made his character completely frightening in the second half of the movie.

Pitt's Popularity Grows

After the releases of *Legends of the Fall, Interview with the Vampire,* and *Seven,* it was clear that Pitt's star was solidly in place. In fact, Brad-mania was taking on international proportions. Whether he was in England for a film premiere or Argentina to make a new movie, hysteria broke out when he appeared in public.

Pitt knew that his greatest asset, his attractiveness, could also be his biggest liability if he wasn't careful. He worked hard at choosing roles that let him grow as an actor. He worked himself to near exhaustion, making *Legends* and *Vampire* back-to-back. However, he knew no matter what decisions he made, things would turn out all right. They did, as *Legends* earned $66 million at the box office and *Seven* took in nearly $100 million.

That confidence carried over into his personal life, as he began a serious romance with Paltrow. Their time together helped him adjust to life in the limelight. Paltrow helped him polish his public personality, and he was smart enough to let her guide him. Yet he maintained his down-home spirit by refusing to let the latest acclaim for his talent and looks inflate his ego.

Chapter 5

Downturn

Pitt rode a crest of successful films and a happy private life for most of 1996. He continued to choose offbeat roles he liked and spent his private time in the company of Paltrow. The good times weren't destined to last, however. The next few years would be a struggle for Pitt, both professionally and privately.

Following the critical success of *12 Monkeys*, Pitt joined a star-filled cast in the movie *Sleepers*. His costars included Robert De Niro, Dustin Hoffman, Kevin Bacon, Jason Patric, and Minnie Driver. At first it appeared that a role in the film was a major coup for Pitt. The casting director looked beyond his handsome exterior when deciding to include him in the stellar cast. "Even though

Pitt and Jason Patric in the 1996 film Sleepers. *Despite an all-star cast, the movie was criticized as bland and uninteresting.*

some people label him a pretty boy, I don't see it that way," said Louis DiGiaimo, who cast Pitt in *Sleepers.* "He's got great looks, with soul, and that's what comes across." [41]

In *Sleepers* Pitt plays one of four boys from New York's Hell's Kitchen whose adolescent prank almost kills a man. They are sent to a home for boys, where they are tortured and abused by guards. Years later two of the boys kill the most brutal guard, played by Bacon. Pitt plays the district attorney assigned to prosecute the case. He devises a plan to get his boyhood friends off the hook and get revenge on the other guards.

Despite packing a lot of star power, the movie met with bland reviews when it opened in fall 1996. It was criticized for not being compelling enough to make viewers care about the characters and not interesting enough to keep them from dozing off. The yawner began a streak of nonhits for Pitt.

Working Through Problems

Problems plagued the making of Pitt's next film, *The Devil's Own,* in which he plays an Irish Republican Army gunrunner who befriends an Irish American cop. The film stars perennial movie heartthrob Harrison Ford, who had first come to the public's attention as the appealing scoundrel Han Solo in the first *Star Wars* trilogy. Pitt and Ford were stars of different generations but with the same appealing characteristics. On the surface, pairing them in a film looked like a brilliant casting decision.

Pitt had first seen the script six years earlier and loved the part of antihero Frankie McGuire. The original script called for him to play a dark, drug-abusing character who guns down the inhabitants of a crack house, steals money, and peppers British soldiers with gunfire. It was the type of character Pitt liked because it went against his image. However, there were delays in finding a studio to make the picture, and Pitt's role was softened a great deal when production finally began.

When Columbia agreed to make the film, Pitt suggested Ford for the role of police officer Tom O'Meara, who befriends Pitt's character without realizing he is a terrorist. "I wanted Harrison because, well, I've always loved Harrison," Pitt said. "You get this sense of integrity." [42]

Harrison Ford

Harrison Ford, who played opposite Brad Pitt in *The Devil's Own*, is an established actor with green-gray eyes, rugged features, and a heroic demeanor that consistently draws fans to the box office.

Ford and Pitt have several things in common. Both left college before graduating (Ford failed too many courses to graduate from Ripon College in Wisconsin and left at the end of his senior year), were named *People Weekly's* Sexiest Man Alive, and have veered from the mainstream to establish long and successful careers.

Born on July 13, 1942, Ford is a generation removed from Pitt. But the two stars share a commitment to hard work and a desire to become the best. Ford's career began with small roles in television series and the movie *Dead Heat on a Merry-Go-Round* in 1966, but he almost chose a career as a carpenter when big roles failed to come his way. His first hit movie was George Lucas's *American Graffiti* in 1973.

Ford achieved a minor degree of fame for his role as Han Solo in *Star Wars* in 1977, but his stardom wasn't sealed until he reprised the role three years later in *The Empire Strikes Back*. He went on to star in the action-packed Indiana Jones movies, earn an Oscar nomination for his dramatic performance in *Witness,* and prove he could do comedy in *Working Girl.* He continued to take on roles of heroic, noble men in *Patriot Games, The Fugitive,* and *Clear and Present Danger.*

With two major stars in the film commanding high price tags, there was pressure to get the project done right and make everyone happy. Pitt earned a reported $9 million, while Ford commanded a $20 million salary. The budget of the project ballooned to nearly $100 million.

Troubles began before shooting started. While Pitt was still making *Sleepers,* script rewrites dramatically changed the story he had fallen in love with. Five writers were eventually involved in an extensive overhaul of the script. Instead of shooting British soldiers, Pitt's character sees his own father get shot. He doesn't abuse drugs, and a love interest is added as Pitt's character falls for O'Meara's daughter. Ford's character was dressed up, made more heroic and hardworking, and a scene in which he fumbles his gun was dropped. Pitt stood up for the version of the movie he thought was best. "[Pitt] came in and panicked and said, 'This is not the film I wanted to make,'" said Alan Pakula, who directed the movie. "There were all sorts of reasons to think, 'Wait a minute. This is becoming something else in somebody else's hands.'"[43]

Director Alan Pakula discusses a scene with Pitt and Harrison Ford while shooting The Devil's Own.

When filming began, Ford and Pitt seemed to have different ideas about the movie. With so many script changes, there were long delays in production as writers tinkered with the script. Pitt reportedly became so fed up that he walked off the set. "We had no script," he said. "Well, we had a great script, but it got tossed. It was ridiculous." [44]

Ford was also frustrated by the slow-moving process, but the seasoned actor had seen it happen before. He knew that they would have to finish making the film despite all the production problems and delays. When Columbia threatened to sue, Pitt returned to the set. Once he saw that he had to make the movie, he gave it his all. "Once Brad was committed to this film he worked his tail off," Pakula said. "He pulled it off." [45]

Pitt didn't stop trying to make the best movie he could, no matter how tiring and trying that was. Debates continued throughout the shooting, as Pitt and Ford were obsessed with their characters and often disagreed on how scenes should be played. But Pitt said he and Ford got along fine. It was the hardest film Pitt had ever worked on, yet he realized everyone was trying to make the best movie they could despite the difficult circumstances that surrounded filming. Pitt denied rumors that egos were out of control and that people hid out in their trailers.

Just before the film was finally released, Pitt committed a public relations faux pas that worried everyone involved. He admitted he had been unhappy during filming. He told *Newsweek,* "It was the most irresponsible bit of filmmaking—if you can even call it that—that I've ever seen."[46] He later said those comments reflected on the history of the film before shooting. "I'm not bashing the film or [Columbia Pictures head] Mark Canton. On the contrary, what resulted from this challenge was hard work and dedication from people I've grown to love and respect, and a film I am very proud of,"[47] he said.

It was a testament to Pitt's star power that the film did well in the opening weekend despite his negative comments. It brought in $16 million at the box office and got some good reviews that indicated that the on-set difficulties didn't carry over to the finished product. While Pitt's acting was applauded, the movie wasn't considered a success. The grim story and a lack of focus kept it from being the blockbuster that had been expected from a production starring Pitt and Ford.

A Bigger Paycheck

Despite less-than-stellar reviews for his recent films, Pitt continued to draw well enough at the box office to command a salary increase. He arrived at the top of Hollywood's A-list when he agreed to make *Meet Joe Black* for $17.5 million. In the film, a remake of the

Pitt and actress Claire Forlani in Meet Joe Black. *Now a huge star, Pitt earned a hefty $17.5 million for his role in the film.*

movie *Death Takes a Holiday,* Pitt plays Death, who gets to go to Earth and falls in love. The role wasn't as gritty or grungy as some of his previous experiences, but the character had an intriguing edge that made it a good choice for Pitt.

As Pitt's professional life was swinging between good and bad times, his private life was sliding. Things seemed solid between Pitt and Paltrow in December 1996, when they announced their engagement. Over the Christmas holidays they traveled to see his family in Missouri, as they had the previous year, and celebrated the announcement at a local Red Lobster. No nuptial date was set, but Paltrow happily wore a diamond and gold band Pitt had designed.

Paltrow left for London in February to make a movie but didn't like to be separated from Pitt for long. When she was in London filming, she sipped coffee on the set from a mug with his picture on it. She would gaze at her engagement ring, a band with a large diamond and three tiny stones, with a wistful look in her eyes. Her feelings for her fiancé were evident, and she would often talk about how she missed Pitt and longed to be with him. When he was able to meet her for a romantic getaway in Paris, they held hands as they walked along the river Seine.

Another Challenging Role

While in the midst of his romance with Paltrow, Pitt traveled to Argentina and Canada to film *Seven Years in Tibet.* Pitt continued to reject roles that flaunted only his good looks, telling *Newsweek* that he doesn't pick roles that reinforce his stud image because "1) It's boring. 2) It's stupid. 3) It's death."[48] He was rich and famous but wanted to respect himself as well.

In *Seven Years in Tibet,* Pitt took on the challenging role of an Austrian climber who befriends the young Dalai Lama during a trek in the Himalayas in the 1940s. The adventurous Pitt was confident he could do well in the role and enjoyed the challenges of learning new skills and traveling to new locations.

The movie was made under difficult conditions. Pitt was flown to mountaintops by helicopter to shoot scenes that re-created the time his character spent climbing the Himalayas. Although Pitt was scared of heights, he learned to enjoy mountain climbing. The weather of-

Seven Years in Tibet *was filmed in the remote Andes Mountains in Argentina. Despite difficult filming conditions, Pitt welcomed the challenge.*

ten delayed filming, but Pitt found that exciting and wild. When the helicopter took him to the top of a mountain to shoot a scene, he was greeted by a glowing wall of blue ice as the helicopter landed on a frozen lake. The experience was exhilarating.

But even in the remote Argentinean locale that was the backdrop for *Tibet,* Pitt was adored. Frenzied girls banged on a window a foot from his table as Pitt tried to enjoy a meal in a local restaurant. Fans chartered buses from Buenos Aires to try to catch a glimpse of Pitt, who stayed in the farming community of Uspallata (population 1,300) in the Andes Mountains. His home away from home had to be guarded around the clock to keep him safe from his fans, who stood outside the walled home chanting, "Ole. Ole. Ole. Ole. Brad Peeeeet."[49]

Spending Time Together

Despite the fact that they were both busy making movies, Pitt and Paltrow tried to see each other every two weeks. When they weren't together, they talked on the phone, running up huge intercontinental phone bills. After filming on her movie ended, Paltrow was eager to be with Pitt and turned down a role in *The*

Avengers so they wouldn't have to be apart over the summer. They planned to make the movie *Duets* together, with Paltrow's father directing.

Pitt was excited about their wedding plans. "I can't wait, man," he said. "Walk down the aisle, wear the ring, kiss the bride. Oh, it's going to be great. Marriage is an amazing thing. And what a compliment: 'You're the one I want to spend the rest of my life with.' Because I'm only going to do it once."[50]

Stars Break Up

By June, however, the romance had ended. One day it seemed the two were madly in love; the next it was over. Although they had recently been seen cuddling at clubs and at the British Oscars, the once-solid relationship had dissolved. A photographer saw a downcast Paltrow being consoled by Pitt after they left a London night spot and made an exit into a waiting white limousine. On June 12, Pitt was hanging out with male friends at a nightclub in New York City, where he was filming *Meet Joe Black*. He didn't appear to be nursing a broken heart as he smiled and had a good time, but others in the crowd noticed that Paltrow wasn't with him.

The breakup came so quickly that some suspected it was a ruse to conceal a secret wedding. But when Paltrow moved out of their apartment and bunked with pal Winona Ryder, it was apparent that the split was for real. On June 16, 1997, Pitt and Paltrow officially split. Pitt's publicist issued a statement saying, "Brad Pitt and Gwyneth Paltrow have mutually agreed to end their two-and-a-half-year relationship."[51]

It was difficult to say who ended the relationship or why it came to a halt. Some said Pitt was commitment-shy; others that it was a joint decision not made because of a single event. There were stories of an affair between Pitt and costar Claire Forlani during the making of *Meet Joe Black*, but Paltrow called those reports false and foolish. She said that Pitt was a man of integrity and goodness and that the rumors were unjust.

Five months after the breakup, Pitt told the *London Times* that the split had not altered his views toward marriage in general. "I'm not anti-marriage," he said. "I want to be a husband and a father.

I will one day wear the ring, the suit, and kiss the bride. It was not meant to be."[52]

He asserted that there was no third party involved in the breakup. He had seen too many people make the mistake of entering into dalliances on film sets to fall prey to that type of behavior himself. He said he had been loyal to Paltrow but felt it best to end the relationship.

Six months after announcing their engagement, Pitt and Paltrow suddenly split up. Paltrow later said that Pitt broke her heart, and it would never be the same.

Pitt showed himself to be a gentleman a year later when he sent Paltrow flowers to congratulate her for winning the Best Actress Oscar for *Shakespeare in Love.* The breakup hit Paltrow hard. Three years after the split, she said Pitt had changed her life. She told *Vanity Fair* he broke her heart, and it would never be the same.

The breakup was another difficult step for Pitt, but he was certain that things would eventually work out for him. He was upbeat about life even though it was taking him through painful times. He called his life tough, crooked, and fantastic at the same time as the difficult times made him a stronger person.

Playgirl Publishes Photos

Another dig at Pitt's happiness came later that summer, as the nude photos of him and Paltrow resurfaced when *Playgirl* published ten pictures in its August issue. Pitt filed suit against the magazine. A judge blocked *Playgirl* from distributing future copies, but subscribers got their issues.

Pitt's less-than-par year was capped by the release of the disappointing *Seven Years in Tibet.* Critics said Pitt failed to give a believable performance as an Austrian mountain climber who becomes a tutor to the Dalai Lama. The film was also criticized because Pitt's character was based on a mountaineer whose real-life Nazi ties were downplayed in the film. Pitt didn't want to get mixed up with politics, however. "Reporters are always asking me what I feel China should do about Tibet. Who cares what I think China should do?" he said. "I'm here for entertainment, basically, when you whittle everything away. I'm a grown man who puts on makeup."[53]

Staying Positive

After a very successful series of films and a happy private life, things took a nasty turn for Pitt in 1997. He made several films that were panned by critics, and his personal life took a downturn as he broke off his engagement with Paltrow.

Pitt didn't let the problems weigh him down. He resigned himself to the fact that life was going to treat him to tough times as well as happiness and viewed it all as a learning experience. The rotten

Pitt's portrayal of an Austrian mountain climber who befriends the Dalai Lama in Seven Years in Tibet *was judged harshly by critics.*

times tested him, and his reaction to them helped him shape and define his life.

Pitt's confidence and optimism didn't leave him during the difficult times. It couldn't have been easy for him and Paltrow to end their romance, but Pitt knew that sometimes the difficult choice is the right one. He also continued to follow his instincts and chose roles that he felt would help him grow as an actor. Although his performances weren't universally loved, he learned from his experiences and was comfortable with the path he had chosen for his career.

Pitt's rise to stardom had come through a good deal of hard work and conscientious decision-making. Because he believed in himself and respected the work he had done, he was able to keep the downturns in his life in perspective. In his heart, he knew he would rebound. "We toil, and we struggle, and every now and then we get to these perfect moments," Pitt told the *New York Daily News*. "That's what life's about. Not about happily ever after and never-ending happiness, but you get to these moments, and that's what keeps you going." [54]

Chapter 6

Happiness

AFTER MORE THAN a decade in the business, Pitt was comfortable with fame. He had always been confident in what he stood for and had gradually learned to deal with the impact of his success. He was more concerned with who he was inside than his physical appearance. When he looked in the mirror, he saw a guy with yellowing teeth and some prominent pores, but it was a face he respected. He had tried to avoid the Hollywood trap of becoming a personality, and that became easier as he matured as an actor.

"I used to think it was easier to be the new kid, but it's not. It's harder. Much harder," Pitt said. "When you become . . . not a veteran in any sense, but when you're in your fifth-year war term, people don't notice you so much." [55]

Pitt had a relaxed attitude that made it easier for him to accept criticism. His thick skin came in handy when *Meet Joe Black* received

Pitt and actor Anthony Hopkins in the movie Meet Joe Black, *which most critics thought was long-winded and overly sentimental.*

less-than-stunning reviews after it was released in January 1998. Some said his performance was engaging, but most critics thought the film was too long and overly sentimental. "*Meet Joe Black* is a fish-out-of-water comedy," *Entertainment Weekly* said. "Some of it is clever and enjoyable, even touching, yet the characters gaze and ponder moistly, as if to inflate each scene to a level of religious significance." [56]

Pitt took the criticism in stride. He had made the movie during his breakup with Paltrow, and the emotional juggernaut he was on at the time affected his acting. The emotions he was experiencing in his relationship had made an impact on his performance. "Movies come along, and you're in a particular place in your life—this is not an excuse—but it always colors your performance," he said. "I can't watch a film without knowing where I was then, what little terrain of life I was going through at that point." [57]

Pitt thought the movie had some beautiful themes of family, love, and dealing with loss. He suspected his acting was judged harshly because he seemed to be a guy who had everything. He felt the pace of the movie was appropriate, even if the two-hour, fifty-minute film got a little long-winded. Even when an artist strives for perfection, he can make a mistake. Although the film had its faults, Pitt didn't think it should have received the critical beating it was subjected to.

Fighting Back

Professionally and personally, things were about to go on an upswing for Pitt. His next movie was the grim, gritty, and edgy *Fight Club*. He again wanted to downplay his romantic side, and the surreal film appealed to his darker impulses. The movie, which also stars Ed Norton, is about a chain of underground clubs where men beat up one another. Pitt again toyed with his good looks. He had the caps removed from his teeth to show the chips he got as a kid, giving him a jagged smile that made his character more realistic. He also shaved his flowing hair.

"I think he suffers—or feels that he suffers—for his great looks," said Laura Ziskin, president of Fox 2000, which made *Fight Club*. "Someone described him as ice cream on the screen. You

Pitt's performance in the violent, edgy film Fight Club *was described by critics as "cool" and "charismatic," and Pitt himself was pleased with his work in the movie.*

can't resist him. But I think his good looks become a motivation for him to do something more daring."[58]

The movie was controversial because of the way it embraced and glorified violence, but it was also a winner for Pitt. Directed by David Fincher, who also directed Pitt in the successful film *Seven*, the movie was described as startling and exhilarating. Pitt plays the charismatic Tyler Durden, who starts up a string of underground fight clubs where men engage in bare-knuckle fighting matches in order to act out their repressed rage. His performance was described as "cool, charismatic and more dynamically physical perhaps than he has been since his breakthrough role in *Thelma and Louise*."[59]

Pitt was happy with his performance. "I think I am better than I have ever been now," Pitt said. "I've seen a progressive growth. You see some of the first stuff I did—it's absolute crap. It's amazing someone let me get in there again. I'm just horrid. Really, really bad. Just no acting clue whatsoever, man. Horrendous. Just phony as phony. And then you start to discover things that feel right."[60]

A Special Friend

In spring 1998 things began to go right in Pitt's personal life as well. He secretly began dating the woman who would become the love of his life. He and Jennifer Aniston, a star of the hit television sitcom *Friends*, had begun noticing each other at celebrity get-togethers. In true Hollywood style, their agents set up their first date, a quiet dinner for two.

Jennifer Aniston

Jennifer Aniston was born on February 11, 1969, in Sherman Oaks, California, and was raised in New York. Her mother, Nancy, was an actress and model, and her father, John, appeared on the soap opera *Days of Our Lives*. Her godfather, Telly Savalas, was the star of *Kojak*. Aniston's parents divorced when she was nine.

Aniston attended New York's High School of the Performing Arts. She appeared in some theater roles after graduating, worked as a waitress, and went to Hollywood. She appeared in several failed television shows, including *Ferris Bueller*, *Molloy*, *The Edge*, and *Muddling Through* and was featured in the thriller *Leprechaun*, which did little to propel her career.

Driven to get better parts, Aniston lost thirty pounds in a year, going from 140 pounds to 110. "It's unfortunate that Hollywood puts pressure on women to be thin," Aniston said. "Because it sends the wrong message."

The sitcom *Friends* brought Aniston fame and fortune. Her role as Rachel led women everywhere to copy her hairstyle. Her movie credits include *She's the One*, *'Til There Was You*, *Picture Perfect*, *Office Space*, and *The Object of My Affection*.

Jennifer Aniston is best-known for her role as Rachel on the successful television sitcom Friends.

The two stars struggled to keep their relationship private. However, public curiosity about the couple made it very difficult for them to maintain the secret. Photographed together at the Tibetan Freedom Concert in Washington, DC, in June 1998, they said they were just pals, but the photo showed them snuggling together.

Still hesitant after his breakup with Paltrow, however, Pitt was reluctant to put a label on their relationship, for fear of jeopardizing it. He didn't know what to tell a reporter when Aniston's name was brought up during an interview in November 1998. Pitt called relationships with women "experiments" but did say he was at a good time in his life.

The couple tried to nurture their relationship outside of the spotlight. They both attended the Manhattan premiere of *Meet Joe Black* but entered and exited the theater separately. They wanted to see if their relationship would grow on its own, without any prodding from the public.

Hoping for Marriage

Pitt's split with Paltrow failed to dim his hopes for someday having a happy marriage. He had grown up in a warm, loving family and could see himself as the patriarch in that scenario. He had many relationships in California but was always very committed. The joy of sharing his life with someone for a lifetime was still a dream he carried with him.

Pitt called love and marriage fantastic and couldn't imagine anything better than being committed to spending his life with another person. He saw marriage as an opportunity for personal growth and was confident he would be a good husband. At the same time, however, he was not in a rush to head to the altar. He wanted to be certain the time was right. He had done a very good job of timing things in his career, so there was no reason for him to direct his personal life any differently.

Spending Time Together

Although they weren't forthcoming about the status of their relationship in public, Pitt and Aniston privately spent plenty of time

together. Pitt flew to Austin to be with Aniston while she was filming the comedy *Office Space* in 1998. Their activities were generally
low-key, such as ordering room service at her hotel and working
out in the gym. While they were dating, Pitt again showed his domestic side, preferring quiet evenings at home to nights out on the
town. They enjoyed barbecuing with friends, watching the television series *The Sopranos,* and hiking. They vacationed together in
Spain, Portugal, and the Sierra Nevadas.

In spring 1999 the romantic Pitt threw two parties for Aniston's
thirtieth birthday. He invited five hundred people, including the
Friends cast, to the hip L.A. restaurant Barfly for a party that included pizza and techno music. The next weekend he chartered a
plane for himself, Aniston, whom he called "my girl," and some
friends. They had a birthday/Valentine's Day celebration at the
Villa Alejandra residence in Acapulco that included fireworks ex-

*Pitt and Aniston attend a Lakers basketball game together. The couple's
romance blossomed for more than a year before they admitted publicly to
their relationship.*

ploding over the Pacific coast. Three buffet tables were brimming with oysters, shrimp, and tropical fruit. The secluded property is set against a towering cliff and opens onto a private beach dotted with coconut shells and palm branches. Pitt and his friends played touch football in the water. Aniston chatted with the other women. They danced and snuggled until 5 A.M. "Whatever they asked for they could get," gardener Enrique Martinez said. "They were kissing everywhere."[61]

Taking Chances

Maybe it was because he was head over heels in love, maybe because he just wanted to do something different, but Pitt continued to show he wasn't afraid to make unusual moves. In the October 1999 issue of *Rolling Stone*, he wore a series of clingy dresses in a photo layout that accompanied a story about him. As a sought-after celebrity, he had done many, many interviews and photo shoots. This time he wanted to do something really different, something that created an alternative world rather than showing him once again as a good-looking guy facing the camera.

Pitt had become savvy about managing his career and spent a lot of time thinking about where he wanted to be. Although he constantly fought against the image of an attractive but brainless country bumpkin, he knew how to keep from getting blinded in the bright lights of Hollywood. He sometimes played up his kind, sweet nature to fool people into thinking he wasn't catching on to things as quickly as the clever Pitt really was.

No longer a naive newcomer, Pitt knew that others did not hold to the same standards he expected of himself. He realized that not everyone had the same values he did. He treated others as he liked to be treated and judged others according to how he expected himself to behave. However, he knew that not everyone adhered to the same rules he did.

Pitt refused to be overwhelmed by his success. Throughout his career, his looks had been his greatest challenge as well as his greatest asset. He had to overcome a stereotype of being good-looking but empty inside and show that he had the character and wisdom to make it in Hollywood. He made sure he chose roles

Despite a successful career and the admiration of millions of fans around the world, Pitt has remained grounded and true to himself.

and made decisions that he could live with. Although he had a successful career and all the material goods he wanted, he realized that he couldn't buy self-respect.

Out in the Open

Pitt and Aniston finally began to open up about their relationship in fall 1999. When they arrived hand in hand at the Emmy Awards on September 12, it was the first opportunity for photographers to get a shot of the couple posing together. Pitt revealed his feelings for Aniston in *Rolling Stone.* "It's called love, I suppose. There's nothing wrong with that. Greatest thing in the world," he said. "She's fantastic, she's complicated, she's wise, she's fair, she has great empathy for others . . . , and she's just so cool."[62]

Engagement rumors flared in late 1999 when Aniston flashed a diamond ring at a Sting concert on November 21. The couple was onstage with Sting when Pitt grabbed Aniston's left hand and pointed at the ring. She smiled as he sang the lyrics to "Fill Her Up," which seemed to confirm the public's suspicions that the engagement was for real. "Up in the front seat a pretty redhead / We're going to Vegas, we're gonna get wed / So fill her up, son, don't be staring / That's a real diamond she be wearing."[63]

At a postshow party at the Shark Bar in Manhattan, the pair kissed and cuddled. When a band member's wife commented on the beautiful ring and asked if they were engaged, Jennifer reportedly said, "Yeah!"

The pair spent a very domestic Christmas together at the home of Pitt's parents. Ever the gentleman, he kept checking to see if she

Pitt and Aniston publicly confirm that they are in love when they arrive hand in hand at the Emmy Awards in Fall 1999.

needed anything, although he declined to join Aniston, his mom, and his sister in the pedicure they were getting at home.

Wedding Plans

For months family, friends, and the pair's publicists denied knowing anything about an impending wedding. But in late July word leaked out: Pitt, thirty-six, and Aniston, thirty-one, were planning to marry on July 29, 2000.

The wedding was held on television producer Marcy Carsey's ocean-side estate in Malibu, California. Photographers, TV cameras, and news helicopters checked out the wedding site for a week before the event, and Pitt and Aniston got officials to declare a no-fly zone around the estate to keep photographers from getting a shot from the air. Part of California's Pacific Coast Highway was shut down on the day of the event to prevent people from peering in.

A Wedding to Remember

On a sunny Saturday afternoon, two hundred guests arrived for the seaside ceremony. *Friends* cast members Courteney Cox Arquette,

Unusual Dreams

A dream about people using his toothbrush has followed Pitt throughout his career. In a 1992 interview with Jay Martel, Pitt revealed in *Rolling Stone* that for five nights in a row he had dreamed that someone wanted to borrow his toothbrush. "It's a different person in each dream," he said. "I just watch them brushing their teeth with my toothbrush and cringe."

Perhaps Pitt was still getting used to his fame and the toothbrush dream symbolized the fact that he was uncomfortable with strangers knowing the intimate details of his life. Or maybe he feared getting taken advantage of by strangers or was obsessed by hygiene. Whatever the reason, the dream persisted.

In a 1999 interview with Chris Heath, also for a *Rolling Stone* article, Pitt said the ending to the dream had changed. "A couple of years ago I started having a dream that someone used my toothbrush," he said, "but that I had all these other toothbrushes at my disposal and I didn't know I had them."

Perhaps Pitt was feeling more comfortable with his star status and the new ending to the dream reflected his ability to be in control. He felt the dream dealt with his feelings toward fame and revealed that he was also having comedy dreams that sometimes made him laugh in his sleep. He was at a happy time in his life, and his feelings were reflected in his subconscious.

A huge tent was erected at Marcy Carsey's ocean-side estate in Malibu to conceal the Pitt-Aniston wedding from unwanted news reporters and paparazzi.

Lisa Kudrow, Matthew Perry, and David Schwimmer were there, although Matt LeBlanc was filming a movie in a foreign country and couldn't attend. Other guests included Pitt's *Fight Club* costar Edward Norton, Cameron Diaz, and Salma Hayek.

Guests sipped iced tea and punch while a string quartet played classical music as a prelude to the 6:30 P.M. ceremony. A forty-member gospel choir sang "Love Is the Greatest Thing" before two bridesmaids, a ring bearer, and flower girls blowing bubbles preceded Aniston down the aisle.

All guests gazed in awe as Aniston walked down the aisle in a floor-length glass-beaded white gown made of satin and silk. The low-backed dress was designed by Lawrence Steele. A circular veil fell gracefully from a crown of pearls and crystal. On her feet were custom ivory-colored, suede high-heel sandals by shoemaker Manolo Blahnik. She carried a bouquet of Dutch Vendela roses so fresh they looked as if she had just plucked them from a garden. The bridesmaids wore green silk chiffon slip dresses with pale taffeta mules, while the flower girls were dressed in cream silk. Pitt

Guests who attended the wedding were treated to an elegant, elaborate celebration, that Pitt later called "the greatest night of my life."

wore a traditional black tuxedo and was flanked by his best man, brother Doug, and groomsman, his father.

The couple first exchanged vows that were both practical and lighthearted. Pitt promised to "split the difference on the thermometer," while his bride vowed she would always make his "favorite banana milk shake." When Aniston missed her cue for the more serious, traditional vows they said together, she exclaimed with perfect timing, "Oh! I've never done this before!" before sealing their union by reciting with Pitt, "With this ring, I thee wed, so that all the world may know my love for you." [64]

Pitt and Aniston spared no expense in making their wedding an elegant celebration for their guests to remember. The grounds were decorated with fifty thousand roses, wisteria, tulips, and other flowers, including lotus flowers floating in a specially built slate fountain. The romantic atmosphere was heightened by the candles made from brown sugar that flickered in the reception tent. Music was provided by four bands, including the Latin jazz group Gypsy Magic. Guests dined on lobster, peppercorn beef, crab, and risotto and pasta. The evening was capped by a fireworks display set to songs by Radiohead, Garbage, and Jeff Buckley.

The elaborate wedding reportedly cost $1 million, including $75,000 for flowers, $300,000 for catering, $100,000 for entertainment, $85,000 to lodge out-of-town guests, and $20,000 for the fireworks that ended with a heart-shaped display over the Pacific. The budget also included $100,000 for security, a necessity after Pitt's home was broken into by an avid fan earlier in the year. Guests had to wear pearl pins to get past security guards.

The evening also included the traditional bouquet toss and garter throw, which was accomplished after Pitt removed Aniston's garter with his teeth. They then cut the six-tier wedding cake. The pair enjoyed the event, right up to the cake tasting. "They were looking into each other's eyes when they fed it to each other and they were laughing with cake in their mouths,"[65] said Dakota Horvath, a twelve-year-old singer who performed at the wedding.

Pitt hadn't been keen on such a showy wedding at first, but after the ceremony he was very happy they had gone the extravagant route. "I was pushing for elopement," Pitt told the *New York Daily News*. "But the ceremony turned out to be extraordinary. It was the greatest night of my life."[66]

Back to Work

Pitt couldn't bask in the romantic afterglow of the wedding for long. Soon he was back at work, shooting the movie *The Mexican* with Julia Roberts, playing an outlaw whose gun is supposedly cursed. In September Pitt attended the London premiere of his movie *Snatch*. The crowd was so excited as Pitt walked down the red carpet that it surged forward. Pitt responded to the crowd's enthusiasm with friendly handshakes and was so amiable that police threatened to arrest him if he didn't get into the theater before pandemonium broke out.

Part of a large cast in the jewel heist caper *Snatch*, Pitt plays Mickey O'Neil. Alluding to both his *Fight Club* and *Devil's Own* characters, Pitt plays an Irish boxer with a scruffy beard. Early reviews of the film were positive. "Pitt has considerable fun in a comic riff on his *Fight Club* persona,"[67] a *Variety* reviewer wrote.

Sexiest Man Again

Pitt's marriage to Aniston only made him more appealing in the eyes of his fans. For the second time, his looks, charm, and confi-

A Star in Mexico

Having Brad Pitt and Julia Roberts in town to film *The Mexican* was a boost to the small Mexican village of Real de Catorce. The remote nineteenth-century silver mining center is connected to the world by a two-mile one-way tunnel and a cobblestone road that winds through the high desert.

Silver was discovered in the town in 1773, an event that swelled its population to more than forty thousand. However, the town that boasted an opera house and silver coin mint saw its population dwindle after the silver was mined out.

Now home to about two thousand people, Real de Catorce had only one phone line before the movie was made. However, Pitt was a famous figure in the village. The bright orange shirts he wore while roaming Real's ruins became highly sought-after items.

Pitt and Julia Roberts during filming of The Mexican *in the remote Mexican village of Real de Catorce.*

Pitt portrays a scruffy Irish boxer in the jewel heist caper Snatch.

dence earned him the title of *People Weekly's* Sexiest Man Alive. Gone was the indecision of Pitt's youth. His commitment made him even more desirable. "Marrying Jennifer was the pinnacle for him," said Marcia Gay Harden, who costarred with Pitt in *Meet Joe Black.* "Sexiness isn't just about the single bachelor and his good looks. There's something gorgeous about his commitment."[68]

Confidence a Key to Pitt's Success

Throughout his career, Pitt has displayed a strong sense of the self-confidence needed to thrive in Hollywood. He has taken every opportunity to grow as an actor, while maintaining an openness and a sense of decency. He has always been confident things will turn out for the best.

After more than ten years in the business, Pitt was comfortable with fame and knew how to deal with his success. The movie *Fight Club* was another edgy choice for the actor, but this time his gamble paid off with a solid performance and some critical praise. His personal life hit a new high as he met Aniston and married her after more than two years of courtship.

Pitt went from bit roles on TV to stud status thanks to his steamy role in *Thelma and Louise.* He has built a loyal following with gritty roles, peppered with turns as good-looking men headed for trouble. His private life has been built on a series of relationships that keep photographers on edge. Throughout his career he has managed to use his good looks to his advantage when he needs to and harness them to further his acting career. He has never lost the boyhood values that are important to him, and he has built a successful and enduring career as one of the most sought-after actors in Hollywood.

Notes

Chapter 1: Solid Foundation

1. Quoted in Chris Mundy, "Slippin Around on the Road with Brad Pitt," *Rolling Stone*, December 1, 1994, p. 94.
2. Quoted in Pam Lambert, "A Legend to Fall For," *People Weekly*, January 30, 1995, p. 56.
3. Quoted in Mundy, "Slippin Around," p. 94.
4. Quoted in Mal Vincent, "Hollywood's Golden Boy Tried to Do Something Different with *Seven*," Knight-Ridder/Tribune News Service, September 21, 1995.
5. Quoted in Alison Powell, "Brad Pitt," *Interview*, February 1992, p. 104.
6. Quoted in Cathy Horyn, "A Commanding Lead," *Vanity Fair*, November 1998, p. 289.
7. Quoted in Chris Heath, "The Unbearable Bradness of Being," *Rolling Stone*, October 28, 1999, p. 69.
8. Quoted in Karen Schneider et al., "The Sexiest Man Alive 2000," *People Weekly*, November 13, 2000, p. 79.
9. Quoted in Jancee Dunn, "Rebel Star Top Dog Brad Pitt," *Rolling Stone*, April 3, 1997, p. 43.
10. Quoted in Deborah Diamond, "Brad, Do Your Homework," *Ladies' Home Journal*, May 1995, p. 59.
11. Quoted in Michelle Burke and Deborah Diamond, "Mad About Brad: I Knew Him Before He Was Hollywood's Hottest," *Ladies' Home Journal*, May 1995, p. 56.
12. Quoted in Lambert, "A Legend to Fall For," p. 56.

93

Chapter 2: Midwestern Kid in Hollywood

13. Quoted in Vincent, "Hollywood's Golden Boy."
14. Quoted in Mundy, "Slippin Around," p. 94.
15. Quoted in Schneider et al., "Sexiest Man Alive 2000," p. 79.
16. Quoted in Schneider et al., "Sexiest Man Alive 2000," p. 80.
17. Quoted in Lambert, "A Legend to Fall For," p. 56.
18. David Hiltbrand, review of *Glory Days, People Weekly,* July 30, 1990, p. 9.
19. Quoted in Jay Martel, "Hot Actor," *Rolling Stone,* May 14, 1992, p. 54.
20. Quoted in Martel, "Hot Actor," p. 56.

Chapter 3: In Charge

21. Jay Robert Nash, *The Motion Picture Guide, 1992 Annual.* New York: Baseline II, 1992, p. 1.
22. Quoted in Martel, "Hot Actor," p. 59.
23. Quoted in James Kaplan, "Brad: Influence," *Entertainment Weekly,* November 6, 1992, p. 30.
24. Quoted in Horyn, "A Commanding Lead," p. 318.
25. Quoted in Kaplan, "Brad: Influence," p. 30.
26. Owen Gleiberman, review of *Kalifornia, Entertainment Weekly,* September 10, 1993, p. 48.
27. Quoted in Josh Mooney, "Brad Pitt: Thief of Hearts," *Cosmopolitan,* November 1995, p. 204.

Chapter 4: Success

28. Quoted in Lambert, "A Legend to Fall For," p. 56.
29. Brian D. Johnson, review of *Legends of the Fall, Maclean's,* January 23, 1995, p. 59.
30. Leah Rozen, review of *Legends of the Fall, People Weekly,* December 19, 1994, p. 23.
31. Quoted in Kimberly Potts, "A Brad-to-the-Bone Look at Hollywood's Sexiest Star," www.eonline.com/Features/Features/Pitt/.
32. Richard Alleva, review of *Interview with the Vampire, Commonweal,* December 16, 1994, p. 16.
33. Quoted in "Brad Pitt: Proving He's in for a Long Run, This

Sex Symbol Slays 'Em at the Box Office," *People Weekly (Special Double Issue: The 25 Most Intriguing People of the Year)*, December 25, 1995, p. 78.

34. Quoted in Vincent, "Hollywood's Golden Boy."

35. Quoted in Dunn, "Rebel Star," p. 42.

36. Quoted in Tom Gliatto et al., "Love Lost," *People Weekly*, June 30, 1997, p. 80.

37. Quoted in Karen S. Schneider, "Look Who Bagged Brad," *People Weekly*, January 15, 1996, p. 64.

38. Quoted in Mary Bruno, "Brad & Gwyneth & Their Monday-Morning Tabloids," www.mrshowbiz.go.com/archive/news/Todays_Stories/960410/4_1996.html, April 10, 1996.

39. Quoted in Mooney, "Brad Pitt," p. 204.

40. Quoted in Schneider, "Look Who Bagged Brad," p. 64.

Chapter 5: Downturn

41. Quoted in "50 Most Beautiful People," www.people/50most/1997/brad.html.

42. Quoted in Degan Pener, "Dealing with the Devil," *Entertainment Weekly*, April 11, 1997, p. 32.

43. Quoted in Pener, "Dealing with the Devil," p. 32.

44. Quoted in Chris Nashawaty, "Devil Dogged," *Entertainment Weekly*, July 12, 1996, p. 8.

45. Quoted in Nashawaty, "Devil Dogged," p. 8.

46. Quoted in Jeff Giles, "Cool. Excellent. Thanks," *Newsweek*, February 3, 1997, p. 50.

47. Quoted in "Brad Pitt Has *Devil* of a Time," www.mrshowbiz.go.com/archive/news/Todays_Stories/970128/1_28/97/3pitt.html, January 28, 1997.

48. Quoted in Giles, "Cool," p. 50.

49. Quoted in Jeff Giles, "A Star's Trek," *Newsweek*, February 3, 1997, p. 48.

50. Quoted in Dunn, "Rebel Star," p. 41.

51. Quoted in Potts, "A Brad-to-the-Bone Look."

52. Quoted in "Brad Pitt on Marriage and Cheating," www.mrshowbiz.go.com/archive/news/Todays_Stories/971104/pitt/11497, November 4, 1997.

53. Quoted in Potts, "A Brad-to-the-Bone Look."
54. Quoted in "Pitt Faces Reality," www.mrshowbiz.go.com/archive/news/Todays_Stories/981110/Pitt111098.html, November 10, 1998.

Chapter 6: Happiness

55. Quoted in Zoe Heller, "Walking the Walk," *Harper's Bazaar,* November 1998, p. 232.
56. Owen Gleiberman, review of *Meet Joe Black, Entertainment Weekly,* November 27, 1998, p. 56.
57. Quoted in Heller, "Walking the Walk," p. 232.
58. Quoted in Horyn, "A Commanding Lead," p. 319.
59. David Rooney, review of *Fight Club, Variety,* September 13, 1999, p. 47.
60. Quoted in Heath, "The Unbearable Bradness of Being," p. 116.
61. Quoted in "Brad and *Friend,*" www.people.com/990308/features/pitt.html, March 8, 1999.
62. Quoted in Heath, "The Unbearable Bradness of Being," p. 68.
63. Quoted in "Rock Solid," www.people.com/991206/features.pitt.html, December 6, 1999.
64. Quoted in Anne-Marie O'Neill, "Isn't It Romantic?" *People Weekly,* August 14, 2000, p. 118.
65. Quoted in O'Neill, "Isn't It Romantic?" p. 126.
66. Quoted in Stephen Silverman, "Brad, Jennifer Go Public," www.people.aol.com/people/daily/story/0,5247,52587,00.html, August 14, 2000.
67. Derek Elley, review of *Snatch, Variety,* September 25, 2000, p. 59.
68. Quoted in Schneider et al., "The Sexiest Man Alive 2000," p. 78.

Important Dates in the Life of Brad Pitt

1963
William Bradley Pitt is born on December 18, 1963, in Shawnee, Oklahoma.

1982
Pitt graduates from Kickapoo High School in Springfield, Missouri, and begins college at the University of Missouri.

1986
Realizing that he won't be able to graduate in the spring, Pitt opts to leave Missouri and try his luck in Hollywood. His first jobs include dressing as a chicken and chauffeuring strippers. He takes acting classes and by fall has landed small acting roles.

1987
Pitt dates Robin Givens after meeting her on the set of the sitcom *Head of the Class.* He also lands a recurring role on *Dallas.*

1988
Yugoslavia is the setting for Pitt's first feature film *The Dark Side of the Sun.* Back in the United States he makes the television movie *A Stoning in Fulham County.*

1989
The slasher movie *Cutting Class* is released, featuring Pitt and Jill Schoelen. Pitt also has a small role in *Happy Together* and he makes *Across the Tracks* with Rick Schroder.

1990

Pitt plays a journalist in the short-lived television series *Glory Days*. He meets Juliette Lewis on the set of the NBC movie *Too Young to Die* and begins a serious relationship with her.

1991

Fame finds Pitt after he steams up the screen with Geena Davis in *Thelma and Louise*. Pitt also makes *The Favor* with Elizabeth McGovern.

1992

Director Robert Redford chooses Pitt for *A River Runs Through It*. Pitt also acts in *Cool World* and *Johnny Suede*.

1993

Gritty roles in *True Romance* and *Kalifornia* help Pitt break away from his handsome image.

1994

Two major movies help solidify Pitt's career: *Legends of the Fall* and *Interview with the Vampire*.

1995

People Weekly names Pitt the Sexiest Man Alive. He earns a Golden Globe and an Oscar nomination for *12 Monkeys*. On the set of *Seven*, he meets Gwyneth Paltrow and begins a two-and-a-half-year relationship.

1996

Pitt is part of a star-filled cast in *Sleepers*.

1997

Pitt's films *The Devil's Own* and *Seven Years in Tibet* are released. Pitt's romance with Paltrow ends with a broken engagement in June.

1998

A streak of nonhits continues for Pitt, as the lengthy *Meet Joe Black* garners little acclaim. Things turn around for Pitt in the spring as he begins dating Jennifer Aniston, his future wife.

1999

Fight Club, starring Pitt and Edward Norton, brings praise for Pitt.

2000

The long-anticipated marriage between Pitt and Aniston takes place on July 29. Pitt makes *Snatch* and *The Mexican* and is slated to appear in *Ocean's Eleven.*

For Further Reading

Books

Amy Dempsey, *Brad Pitt*. Philadelphia: Chelsea House, 1998. An overview of Pitt's life and career.

Holly George-Warren, ed., *Brad Pitt*. Boston: Little, Brown, 1997. Profiles, interviews, and movie reviews, plus seventy-five photos of the actor.

Brian J. Robb, *Brad Pitt: The Rise to Stardom*. London: Plexus, 1996. A detailed look at Pitt's early career.

Periodicals

Tom Gliatto et al., "Love Lost," *People Weekly*, June 30, 1997.

Cathy Horyn, "A Commanding Lead," *Vanity Fair*, November 1998.

Pam Lambert, "A Legend to Fall For," *People Weekly*, January 30, 1995.

Josh Mooney, "Brad Pitt: Thief of Hearts," *Cosmopolitan*, November 1995.

Chris Mundy, "Slippin Around on the Road with Brad Pitt," *Rolling Stone*, December 1, 1994.

Anne-Marie O'Neill, "Isn't It Romantic?" *People Weekly*, August 14, 2000.

Degan Pener, "Dealing with the Devil," *Entertainment Weekly*, April 11, 1997.

Karen Schneider et al., "The Sexiest Man Alive 2000," *People Weekly*, November 13, 2000.

Internet Sources

Kimberly Potts, "A Brad-to-the-Bone Look at Hollywood's Sexiest Star," www.eonline.com/Features/Features/Pitt/. A clever, sometimes cheeky account of the highlights of Pitt's career and personal life.

www.mrshowbiz.go.com/people/bradpitt/index.html. A brief bio and the latest news stories about Pitt.

www.people.com. News and archive information on Pitt and other celebrities.

Works Consulted

Books

Jay Robert Nash, *The Motion Picture Guide, 1992 Annual*. New York: Baseline II, 1992.

Periodicals

Richard Alleva, review of *Interview with the Vampire, Commonweal,* December 16, 1994.

"Brad Pitt," *Current Biography,* March 1996, p. 32.

"Brad Pitt: Proving He's in for a Long Run, This Sex Symbol Slays 'Em at the Box Office," *People Weekly (Special Double Issue: The 25 Most Intriguing People of the Year),* December 25, 1995.

Michelle Burke and Deborah Diamond, "Mad About Brad: I Knew Him Before He Was Hollywood's Hottest," *Ladies' Home Journal,* May 1995.

Deborah Diamond, "Brad, Do Your Homework," *Ladies' Home Journal,* May 1995.

Jancee Dunn, "Rebel Star Top Dog Brad Pitt," *Rolling Stone,* April 3, 1997.

Derek Elley, review of *Snatch, Variety,* September 25, 2000.

Mitchell Fink, "Jennifer in Love," *Redbook,* August 1999.

Jeff Giles, "Cool. Excellent. Thanks," *Newsweek,* February 3, 1997.

———, "A Star's Trek," *Newsweek,* February 3, 1997.

Owen Gleiberman, review of *The Favor, Entertainment Weekly,* May 13, 1994.

————, review of *Kalifornia*, *Entertainment Weekly*, September 10, 1993.

————, review of *Meet Joe Black*, *Entertainment Weekly*, November 27, 1998.

————, review of *Seven*, *Entertainment Weekly*, September 29, 1995.

Chris Heath, "The Unbearable Bradness of Being," *Rolling Stone*, October 28, 1999.

Zoe Heller, "Walking the Walk," *Harper's Bazaar*, November 1998.

Brian D. Johnson, review of *Legends of the Fall*, *Maclean's*, January 23, 1995.

James Kaplan, "Brad: Influence," *Entertainment Weekly*, November 6, 1992.

Jennifer Kornreich, "Hollywood in Love," *Ladies' Home Journal*, September 2000.

Jay Martel, "Hot Actor," *Rolling Stone*, May 14, 1992.

Chris Nashawaty, "Devil Dogged," *Entertainment Weekly*, July 12, 1996.

Alison Powell, "Brad Pitt," *Interview*, February 1992.

David Rooney, review of *Fight Club*, *Variety*, September 13, 1999.

Leah Rozen, review of *Legends of the Fall*, *People Weekly*, December 19, 1994.

Karen S. Schneider, "Look Who Bagged Brad," *People Weekly*, January 15, 1996.

Mal Vincent, "Hollywood's Golden Boy Tried to Do Something Different with *Seven*," Knight-Ridder/Tribune News Service, September 21, 1995.

Internet Sources

"Brad and *Friend*," www.people.com/990308/features/pitt.html, March 8, 1999.

"Brad Pitt Has *Devil* of a Time," www.mrshowbiz.go.com/archive/news/Todays_Stories/970128/1_28/97/3pitt.html, January 28, 1997.

"Brad Pitt on Marriage and Cheating," www.mrshowbiz.go.com/
archive/news/Todays_Stories/971104/pitt/11497, November 4,
1997.

Mary Bruno, "Brad & Gwyneth & Their Monday-Morning Tabloids"
www.mrshowbiz.go.com/archive/news/Todays_Stories/960410/
4_1996.html, April 10, 1996.

"50 Most Beautiful People,"www.people.com/50most/1997/brad.
html, May 12, 1997.

"Pitt Faces Reality," www.mrshowbiz.go.com/archive/news/Todays_
Stories/981110/Pitt111098.html, November 10, 1998.

"Rock Solid," www.people.com/991206/features.pitt.html, December
6, 1999.

Stephen Silverman, "Brad, Jennifer Go Public," www.people.aol.
com/people/daily/story/0,5247,52587,00.html, August 14, 2000.

Index

Picture Credits

Cover photo: © Gary Marshall/Shooting Star
© AFP/CORBIS, 58
AP Photo/DreamWorks, Merrick Morton, 90
AP Photo/La Nacion, Alejandro Querol, 47
AP Photo/Mark J. Terrill, 11
AP Photo/Mark J. Terrill, Pool, 88
© Morton Beebe, S.F./CORBIS, 24
ClassMates.Com Yearbook Archives, 19, 20
Fotos International/Archive Photos, 71
Fotos International/Max Miller/Archive Photos, 49
Fotos International/Peter Sorel/Archive Photos, 57
© Mitchell Gerber/CORBIS, 54
© Dave G. Houser/CORBIS, 13
Photofest, 9, 17, 23, 27, 29, 31, 32, 35, 36, 39, 40, 41, 42, 43, 45,
    48, 51, 53, 62, 65, 69, 75, 77, 79, 80, 91
Press Association/Archive Photos, 59
Reuters/Lee Celano/Archive Photos, 73
Reuters/FLS/Archive Photos, 68
Reuters/Sam Mircovich/Archive Photos, 87
© Reuters NewMedia Inc./CORBIS, 82, 84, 85

About the Author

Terri Dougherty is a freelance writer from Appleton, Wisconsin. In addition to nonfiction books for children, she also writes magazine and newspaper articles. A native of Black Creek, Wisconsin, Terri graduated from the University of Wisconsin-Oshkosh. She was a reporter and editor at the *Oshkosh Northwestern* daily newspaper for five years before beginning her freelance writing career. In her spare time, Terri plays soccer and reads. She enjoys cross-country skiing and attending plays with her husband, Denis, and swimming, biking, and playing with their three children—Kyle, Rachel, and Emily.